MODERN MASTERS OF THE KEYBOARD

Photo. Kubey-Rembrandt Studios, Phila., Pa.

SERGEI RACHMANINOFF

MODERN MASTERS
OF THE KEYBOARD

BY *Moore*

HARRIETTE BROWER

WITH SIXTEEN PORTRAITS

Essay Index Reprint Series

BOOKS FOR LIBRARIES PRESS

FREEPORT, NEW YORK

First Published 1926
Reprinted 1969

STANDARD BOOK NUMBER:
8369-1124-5

LIBRARY OF CONGRESS CATALOG CARD NUMBER:
70-86736

PRINTED IN THE UNITED STATES OF AMERICA

PRELUDE

The opportunity to confer with so many distinguished artists has given me keen pleasure, as well as information of great value. My questions to them always had in view the needs of the teacher and also the aims of the pianist.

In collecting the following interviews, many of which have already appeared in magazines, I found they required editing and enlarging, which fortunately could be done through longer acquaintance with the artists.

It must be borne in mind that these familiar Talks were taken without notes of any kind, and were written down later from memory. In a number of instances the artists have sent unsolicited letters attesting their approval of the result.

The favor with which *Piano Mastery,* First and Second Series, has been received, and the desire to be of service to the great army of American teachers and players, has inspired the publication of a Third Series of Piano Interviews.

HARRIETTE BROWER.

CONTENTS

vii

viii   *Contents*

ILLUSTRATIONS

MODERN MASTERS OF THE KEYBOARD

MODERN MASTERS OF THE KEYBOARD

I

SERGEI RACHMANINOFF

SERIOUS PIANO PRACTISE A NECESSITY IN AMERICA

"RACHMANINOFF! The man whose art is as pure gold; the sincere artist, equally admired by musicians and the public. He is indeed simple, unassuming, truthful, generous."

These words of Josef Hofmann are a high estimate of one artist by another of great renown.

Sergei Rachmaninoff, composer and pianist, whose art was so much admired on his first visit to America, in 1909-10, has been for several years a resident of this country; he has made his home here, living in the metropolis in winter and voyaging to the other side in summer. During each season he is active in the concert field, bringing his polished art to music lovers in many cities, from coast to coast. His reserved yet intense personality seems to exert a peculiar fascination on the crowded audiences which always greet him.

WHAT IS THE SPELL?

For here is no spectacular exhibition of mere piano virtuosity, no long-haired sensation. The great Russian comes upon the platform with most serious mien and seats himself at the instrument as though quite unaware of the audience, waiting in breathless expectancy for the piano to awake under his touch. His tall figure bends over the keyboard, as he sits a few seconds in utter stillness before beginning. Then his large hands, with their long, shapely fingers, find the desired keys with no perceptible effort, and weave for the listener enchanting pictures, now bright, now sad and filled with longing. Yet Rachmaninoff is not a pianist who wears his heart upon his sleeve; he is always reserved, self-contained, wrapt in serious thought, or so it seems. And each year when he reappears, his art has ripened, his vision is broader, more searching, comprehensive and vital.

The boy Sergei very early showed signs of sympathy with and feeling for music. Even in his fourth year this aptitude was observed by his mother, who began to teach him the piano, and continued to do so until he was nine, when an efficient woman pianist and teacher carried the work further. These two early teachers laid the foundation of the musical structure, which gradually rose later to such imposing proportions.

In 1882 the family moved to St. Petersburg, and the boy was at once placed in the Conservatory, where he studied industriously for three years. Then came another move, this time to Moscow, where the lad had the advantages of the great Conservatory and the musical atmosphere of this exceptional musical center. As he himself puts it: "My grandfather was a notable pianist, my cousin, Alexander Siloti, was one of Liszt's pupils and is still a prominent figure among present-day Russian musicians. Thus my boyhood was spent among musicians and in a musical atmosphere."

It is said that Rachmaninoff belonged to the old aristocratic order in Russia. The grandfather did not play professionally, but there is a tradition that the art of the elder musician has never been surpassed by the pianistic art of the younger.

And this younger Rachmaninoff, now a man of genius, a pianist of the highest attainments, a composer of numerous works for his chosen in-

strument, for voice and orchestra, a conductor
of renown, is living quietly among us here in the
new world. The public knows him as composer-
pianist, and many young people all over the land
struggle to play his famous Prelude in C sharp
minor, or perhaps the later one in G minor. But
the public has no part in his home life: that is
sacred. Few interviewers ever cross the threshold, for it is known that he has an inborn dis-
like to have his privacy invaded.

It had long been an ardent desire of mine to
gain a more intimate view of this distinguished
musician than could be obtained from across the
footlights. I wanted to speak with him face to
face, to inquire his ideas of music study and practise. But season after season passed without my
wish coming any nearer fulfillment. Then, suddenly, one day the summons came to go to him.

The handsome residence, which is the home of
the Russian master, is situated on Riverside
Drive, and overlooks a wide expanse of the Hudson with the Palisades beyond. From midday
until late afternoon—on fine days—the rooms
are flooded with sunshine, turning everything to
gold.

One feels a sense of peace and quietude on
entering this abode. The colors of furnishings
are soft and rich, in artistic blues and deep reds.

Floors and stairways are covered with thick, soft velvets, upon which footfalls are noiseless. As we ascend the stairs, sounds of a piano come floating down to us. The master is playing, or rather is at work on some knotty passage which he repeats over and over with the utmost patience. As we enter he rises to greet us with kindly manner, but with grave, austere expression, as though loath to be disturbed, or to leave the musical train of thought, even for a few moments.

DAILY PRACTISE

To the question as to how the artist keeps his technic in repair and up to concert pitch, he said: "The pianist must play much technic and many technical exercises outside of pieces. He has been trained to do so, for he started out with this idea and these principles from the beginning— that is, if he is a Russian. In my native country music is taught much more thoroughly than it is in America. When a student enters the Conservatory in Russia, he is expected to remain nine or ten years. If talented and able to work quickly, he may be able to cover the ground in eight years, though this is seldom done. Of course, you understand he takes other studies along with music: history, literature, languages, philosophy and other subjects.

PURE TECHNIC

"The study of pure technic includes scales, chords, arpeggios, trills and octaves. How can the student expect to learn difficult pieces without a background of technical forms, well digested and mastered? It is perfectly impossible. And if this technical drill and routine are necessary for the student, shall the concert player cast them aside às useless? Not at all; he would be very foolish to do so. If I wish to keep my playing mechanism in condition, I, too, must practise scales, arpeggios, trills, chords and octaves. There is no other way to keep fit.

STUDENTS NOT SUFFICIENTLY SERIOUS

"As I travel over your great country and observe conditions, it seems to me the students of music do not study seriously—not with whole heart and soul. There may be several causes for this condition of things; the entire blame cannot be placed on any one of them. For one thing, there seems to be a lack of good teachers. The best teachers here in America are excellent, but there are too few and they are generally found in the music centers and large cities. Smaller places are obliged to get along with a much poorer quality, though they, too, need the best.

THE NEED OF THE HOUR

"You ask what I consider this country's greatest need, the need of the hour. I answer without hesitation—intelligent, industrious practise. Students of music, in this particular, are indifferent, or, shall I say it frankly? they are downright lazy. They don't give their minds to the work they have taken up—they don't give sufficient time to their studies; they fritter away precious moments and hours on superficial things, instead of devoting their time to mastering the beautiful art they have undertaken to study. Technical mastery of the piano cannot be won in a month or a year; it is the result of many years of ceaseless study. But even if the student does not wish to enter a public career, there is no reason why piano study should not be pursued along correct lines. Why should not the student go thoroughly even a part of the way? If he attempts the study at all, he should bend all his mental powers to the tasks he has set himself.

"As you suggest, there may be some reasons why American pupils are inclined to slight the study of music and become superficial. There are many distractions."

One of these is surely the radio, was remarked, which he agreed could be very distracting, if the whole family were interested in listening to it. And yet it was sadly evident that really good music was all too seldom heard over the radio, which fact was the more unfortunate, he thought, if the students were obliged to listen to much of it.

MODERN MUSIC

"What do I think of modern music? I am free to admit I do not think highly of it. There is very little—indeed but a small proportion of what is composed today—that is attractive or that has any lasting value. What is the use of this constant struggle after originality—of the great effort to dress up the musical idea in unusual form and shape, if the thought itself has little meaning or vitality? Music is a spiritual art; it should elevate and enrich life with beautiful thoughts, feelings and experiences. These vital things seem to be lacking in most modern music.

"The music of MacDowell? He has done interesting things. I am somewhat familiar with the Sonatas and some of the shorter pieces. But his music is not much known abroad, at least not in Russia.

"In Russia we have a number of composers whose works are not known on this side. One of them is Nikolai Medtner, a really great composer. Some have called him the 'Russian Brahms,' yet this a wrong name for him. He is individual and does not pattern after any one else. He is also called a modernist, yet Medtner hates modernism. His music is always true music. Possibly in that sense it is modern, but it never is meaningless and discordant. In addition to being a great composer, Medtner is a wonderful pianist. I trust that when he comes, both his playing and his compositions will be appreciated in America.

"Reverting to American music once more, I would like to say that I recently heard a composition by an American, that pleased me greatly; it really is a fine piece of work. It is in the form of an orchestral Suite and the composer is Deems Taylor. Its title is—as you suggest— *Through the Looking-Glass.* I hope Mr. Taylor has done, or will do, other things, for he has great ability.

"This composition was played by the Philadelphia Orchestra, an extremely fine organization. Indeed, the orchestras of America—the best of them—lead the world in excellence and high ideals.

"America has almost unlimited possibilities and potentialities, and can eventually develop into a great musical nation. You have made immense strides forward ever since I first came here, fifteen years ago. There is really now no necessity for the American student to go abroad for music study, for you have every requisite in your own country for the training and perfecting of great musicians. You have public-spirited men, too, men of wealth, who seem ready and willing to devote their means to the fostering of music and art. There is no doubt that one day you will have a great music school or conservatory, which will train your talented youth to do high things in music, both as executive and creative artists. And I believe it is much better, for many reasons, for the music student to receive his training in his native land, *if* he can only receive training of the right sort. The strength and vitality of your social, home and outdoor life should influence the student in his musical and artistic expression.

"No, I do not teach piano, as I have no time. I shall start very soon on a long tour of several months' duration. My summer vacations I usually spend on the other side. Whenever and wherever there is time and opportunity for quiet thought and study, I turn to composition."

BEGINNERS SHOULD HAVE BEST TEACHERS

In speaking further of the need for good teachers for those just starting in to study music, he said:

"It frequently is affirmed that an indifferent teacher will do just as well to start with. Never was there a greater mistake. The child who shows signs of musical aptitude should be allowed the very best teacher it is possible to secure. Do not place a child of even five years old under a poor, inefficient teacher. Else what is poorly done will have to be done all over again—a difficult matter, for early impressions are most lasting, as we all know.

"It is to be hoped the day will come when there will be no more poor teachers, for they will all be trained for the great work of teaching, and will realize their high calling and wonderful opportunities."

II

MORITZ ROSENTHAL

BUILDING A CONCERT TECHNIC

MORITZ ROSENTHAL is indisputably a true giant of the keyboard. Born in Lemberg, in 1862, he had made such progress under Mikuli, pupil of Chopin and then Director of the Lemberg Conservatory, that he played the Chopin Rondo for two pianos, with his teacher, in public, at the age of ten. Later his parents moved to Vienna and he became a pupil of Joseffy, and the Tausig method. At fourteen he made his début in Vienna, which was followed by a phenomenal tour through Roumania. From 1876 to 1878 he was with Liszt in Weimar and Rome. After making a sensation in Paris and St. Petersburg in 1878, he withdrew from the concert field and devoted himself to classical and philosophical studies, keeping up his piano practise at the same time. When he emerged to continue his concert career, in 1884, he caused amazement by his marvelous technic and endless physical endurance. Since then he has concertized in many parts of

To Mme. Marriotte Brower with kindest regards, Moritz Rosenthal — Jan. 1st 1924

MORITZ ROSENTHAL

the world. Five tours in America have been
made; the fifth one separated about seventeen
years from the fourth.

It was during his last tour that I had the
pleasure of meeting the artist, and conferring
with him on things pertaining to his art.

Just before starting to keep my appointment,
I said to one of my students: "And what shall
I ask the master, when I come face to face with
him?" as I was a bit curious as to how she would
answer.

"Ask him how he has acquired his marvelous
technic," was her reply.

It is a curious fact that to think of Rosenthal
is to think of stupendous technic and great physical endurance. It is said of him that when he
appeared in Vienna, in 1884—he was only
twenty-two then—he astounded his listeners by
his performance, the critics declaring him to be
the greatest living technician. And at first that
is a frequent impression. But it is soon discovered that, in his case, stupendous technic is only
a means to an end, only a legitimate vehicle of
musical expression. It is recognized then that
Rosenthal is a musician of intellectual power
and keen penetration. His playing gives ample
proof of the perfect balance of the technical and
intellectual in whatever he does.

There are some who assert that the sort of technic this pianist employs is of the old-fashioned Leipsic order, the old German school, though brought to highest perfection. They have not observed, perhaps, that the artist at times uses some of the arm-weight movements, which formerly did not belong to that school of piano playing. These movements and conditions aid in the beautiful tones which he generally draws from the instrument. All must agree he is a truly great and unique artist.

Arriving at the appointed hour of my visit, I was shown to the luxurious study occupied by the pianist, in one of the newest uptown hotels. He was at work at the piano as I entered, but rose and received me graciously. Near his grand piano stood his practise keyboard. It was propped up on two chairs, and was rather a thin, simple affair, which was hinged in the middle, and could fold up in order to be tucked away in a trunk or traveling-case. It had no regulated action or touch, and seemed to be just a "dumb keyboard."

"It was made especially for me, to my order," remarked the artist, pressing the keys here and there with his wonderfully developed hands. "Yes, it accompanies me on all my tours," he added.

A CONCERT TECHNIC

"And you want to know how I acquired my technic, or, to put it more impersonally, what are the essentials of a concert technic today?

"It would be very difficult for me to say how and where I acquired my technic, as it has come from many sources, and, latterly, from the study of difficult portions and characteristic passages in pieces.

"First of all, I am not favorable to a great deal of time being given to finger exercises, so called. They can be interminably repeated, *ad nauseam,* without intelligence and without imagination. Such useless repetition is for many pupils as though they were in a boat, rowing aimlessly about, not knowing whither—having no destination. Young people often take up the study of music with no natural ability and no aim in view. It would be more profitable for such students to undertake some other branch of study, as with no innate ability they will only make a failure of music.

"It requires both intelligence and imagination to grasp technical principles and to work them out. Each player's hand is more or less individual, and he must adapt technic to his needs. He must imagine the kind and quality of tone required for every effect, and how to produce and develop that tone to the best advantage. He thus requires both these mental qualities to seize on the right means to develop his technical apparatus, to prepare his tools, if you will, to be used to the highest achievement.

LEGATO TOUCH

"A necessity for the pianist is a correct understanding of the legato touch. In reality we seldom find it understood by the general student. Legato does not mean holding one key tightly till the next is struck, although many players think it does. Artistic legato means that the keys are to be depressed in such a manner and with such a quality of tone that the sounds seem to be connected, even though there may be a very slight separation between them. Imagination here plays a large rôle in securing this result.

TECHNICAL MATERIAL

"In early stages the pupil should naturally learn principles of touch and movements for arm, wrist and fingers, and how to apply them in trills, scales, chords, arpeggios and octaves. For the last—the octaves—I advise both elevated and low wrist, after the manner shown by Kullak in his Octave School.

"When these principles are understood and are somewhat under control, Czerny can be taken up. Here again use intelligence and imagination, and study those études most appropriate to your needs. So, whether it be the School of Velocity, Op. 299, the School of Virtuosity, Op. 740, the School of Legato and Staccato, or any of the other sets—I no longer remember the opus numbers—choose intelligently what is best to study. Through conscientious study of these various forms, you will gain the things necessary for your development. But, if you merely run through them for the sake of practising technic, you will again be like the rudderless boat, aimlessly drifting and arriving nowhere.

"When I have a little leisure—not now, of course, when I am on tour—but at some future time, I intend to write out a set of exercises for the complete development of the hand. The principles of technic thus set down will be illustrated by certain études, which I shall select for the further development of the player. This idea has been in my mind for some years, waiting for time and opportunity to carry it out.

"To continue with our technic building. After Czerny, Clementi, in the Tausig edition, will be found useful in forming a concert technic. This does not mean, I take it, that the student should master every one of the Clementi Études, but only those found to be the most improving and valuable to his own particular development.

"Henselt has put forth some valuable study material, especially in études built on widely extended chords and arpeggios; these are really difficult. Also Moscheles ought not to be forgotten, for there is much good material to improve a concert technic in his collection of Twenty-four Characteristic Studies, Op. 70.

"It is a wide jump from the material I have enumerated to the two books of Études by Chopin. He has taken up the principal technical points, and illustrated them in incomparable studies, such as the Double Thirds, the Études in Sixths and in Octaves, chromatic runs as in Number Two, staccato intervals, as in Number Seven, arpeggio forms, as in the first and last Études, and many other necessary technical points. And while the student is mastering technical difficulties, he is also working on the musical and interpretative side, for both go hand in hand, through the study of these wonderful études. In this way one combines technic study with repertoire. Here one learns to mold beautiful tones, to infuse poetry and feeling into these phrases. And as a result of mastering various kinds of pianistic difficulties, one has also a command of two dozen beautiful compositions, each one unique of its kind.

"As I said a moment ago, the difficult passages in pieces also form excellent material for technical study. There are countless such passages in Chopin and Liszt, so that one need never lack an objective for study. For octave practise it is a good plan to select octave passages from certain pieces, and keep them in constant review. Such, for instance, would be the pages of octaves in Liszt's Sixth Rhapsodie. Or the Finale from the same composer's Fourth Rhapsodie, though I consider this piece inferior to the Sixth. Perhaps this is the reason we so seldom hear it.

MODERN MUSIC

"I am sometimes asked if I am in sympathy with modern music, and if it finds a place on my programs. If 'modern music' really means ultra-modern music, I answer emphatically in the negative. Much of this extremely modern so-called music is poor stuff indeed, lacking in form, shape, melody and harmony. It amazes me that such distortion and cacophony can be set down and performed in the name of music, and that people should ever consider it seriously. There are a few modern composers who have put forth some interesting music for the piano. I play

some Skryabin, though not his later compositions—not beyond Opus 40. I also play some
Albeniz and Debussy, though not a great deal
of the latter.

"But there are worthy modern works that are
unknown, simply for lack of the public's interest,
or of the manager's either. To mention one composer whose work is little known as yet, is to
speak of the Polish master, Xaver Scharwenka.
He has written several concertos which are excellent, but they are seldom heard, and are quite
unknown in America. I consider them finer than
the Saint-Saens concertos. I have proposed the
Fourth Concerto by Scharwenka to orchestral
leaders here, but they refuse to put it on their
programs. I suppose they don't want to take
time to study a new work of that kind.

"It is a great pleasure for me to renew my impressions and friendships in America, as I have
not had the opportunity of doing so for seventeen years. Yes, I find many changes, and great
progress in many ways. And, though the increase in musical knowledge and activities is
marked, yet I had always found, on my previous
visits, a great deal of understanding on musical
subjects. I have never been one to decry the
musical intelligence of this country, for I have
always found appreciation here, and have the

pleasantest recollections of the treatment I have always received in your hospitable land. Before I leave its shores, I must make the trip to California, which will be my fourth visit to the coast."

III

ALFRED CORTOT

PRACTICAL ASPECTS OF MODERN PIANO STUDY

WE have come to know, on this side of the water, the art of the eminent musician, pianist, conductor and teacher of France—Alfred Cortot.

His first American recital took place on Armistice Day, November 11, 1918. While confusion and jubilation reigned in the streets, those who were seated in the concert hall listened quietly to a comprehensive program, beginning with Vivaldi, continuing through Chopin's Andante Spianato and Polonaise, the Twenty-four Preludes entire and some modern French music, on to Liszt's Second Rhapsodie. We recognized, after the first quarter of an hour, that we were listening to one of the great artists of the world. And since that day, each visit he has paid to America has deepened the first impression. Then, too, it is felt that M. Cortot's art has grown and ripened with the years. It has be-

ALFRED CORTOT

come more intense, more vital and sympathetic in touch and tone, more noble in conception.

Alfred Cortot is known to us only as pianist and teacher, but in his own country he has equal renown as conductor, and also as founder of the famous Trio, composed of Jaques Thibaud, violin; Pablo Casals, 'cellist, and himself, pianist, which for a number of years did much for chamber music in France.

The artist's education in piano was gained at the Paris Conservatoire, under Decambes, Rouquon and Diémer. He won First Piano Prize in 1896. Then, after a successful début as pianist in Paris, he went to Baireuth and made a thorough study of Wagner's scores, remaining several years. Returning to Paris, he conducted the first performance of *Götterdammerung,* and subsequently did much, through his orchestral concerts, to increase French appreciation of the works of Richard Wagner.

Cortot's great gifts as master of the piano and its literature made it imperative for him to return to the concert stage, and he has made frequent tours through many countries of the world. He is a distinguished example of the intellectual pianist who does not allow the academic phases of piano study to overbalance his emotional and sympathetic interpretation.

The writer had sought a conference with the French artist during his first American season, but without success. Subsequently, however, in spite of the overwhelming amount of work undertaken by him, the pianist was willing to grant an hour out of his crowded day, to talk over matters of pianistic and pedagogic interest. An appointment was made to meet in his lair—otherwise old Steinway Hall, of blessed memory, fragrant of reminiscences of famous pianists, from Rubinstein down.

Punctual to the minute, M. Cortot appeared, and, with polished French courtesy, led the way to one of the inner rooms, where we would be undisturbed. He assured the visitor he spoke only French, since he has profited by Maeterlinck's experience, and has not tried to learn English "by the phonetic method," at which witty sally we all laughed heartily. As a matter of fact, however, he understands English very well, and can say little sentences in it.

THE TECHNICAL SIDE

"You wish to speak to me about matters pertaining to the technical side of piano playing," began M. Cortot, after he had seen that we were comfortably seated, and he had placed himself on a piano-stool before us. "That is a very important side, especially for the young student. Of course, in the earlier stages, the pupil must be very exact about everything connected with technic—hand position, finger action, relaxation and so on. But, in presenting these fundamental subjects, the student's physique and mentality enter largely into the scheme, so that one might almost say the teacher must have a different method for each pupil. Students cannot all be taught in the same way. I teach in the Conservatoire in Paris, and have ample opportunity to judge of the diversity of gifts. Naturally, I have the advanced students and those especially talented.

"Do not be seated too low at the piano," he went on, continuing the subject we had begun. "The height at which one sits has much to do with tone quality. If one sits too low, and the elbow is below the wrist, the effort to get power often renders the tone harsh; whereas if the arm slopes somewhat down to the wrist, as is the case when one sits higher, the hand and arm are over the keyboard, which fact, of itself, lends weight and strength to the tone."

M. Cortot went to the piano and illustrated his meaning.

ELIMINATE UNNECESSARY PRACTISE

"In the early days, the student has to do considerable technic practise, but the material for this should be so carefully chosen as to eliminate all unnecessary effort. Avoid useless repetition; rather get at the principle—the heart of the thing you want to conquer, and cut away whatever is superfluous. You need practise in scales? Then what is the use of playing them over and over, in rotation, as so many players do. It is only a waste of time. What is the principle of scale playing? Is it not this—putting the thumb under the hand and the hand over the thumb?"

And again the artist turned to the keyboard and played a short exercise, starting on C with thumb, then D with second finger, C again with thumb, B with second finger, and back to C. He illustrated the same principle with other fingers and wider intervals.

"There you have the principle, and it is not necessary to play scales incessantly in order to learn that principle. It is so much better to save one's strength for other things.

"As for variety of material, there is always plenty to be found in pieces. Take the difficult portions and passages of the piece you are studying, one after another, and study them in detail,

each hand alone. Best of all, make new material
for technic practise out of them. For this work,
accents may be varied, rhythms can be changed,
and the passage may, in various ways, be developed in such style as to fix it deeply in the mind,
besides making it valuable for finger, wrist and
arm technic. This manner of study aids concentration and develops the resources of the pupil.
It also does away with the mass of studies and
books of études which some teachers consider so
essential. The pupil realizes he is working on
repertoire, while, at the same time, he is developing and perfecting his technic. Of course, this
especially applies to the advanced worker.

RHYTHM MUST BE INBORN

"I do not consider the metronome at all necessary in piano practise. If used, it is apt to induce mechanical habits. Rhythm must be
inborn; the student must feel the beat, the pulse.
If he is unable to do so, no amount of mechanical
practise will supply this defect."

"Oh, but M. Cortot," we protested. "Just
think of all the young people who love music and
wish to study it—older people, too—who can get
so much pleasure out of a nearer contact with
music, but who may not be blessed with this fine,
inner sense of rhythm. The metronome would

be their only salvation. Through its use they learn what rhythm means. What would they ever do without such an aid and guide?"

"Let them do something else beside music, then," answered the French pianist. "I repeat it—let only those study music who have an innate sense of rhythm. You remember Hans von Bülow's saying, 'In the beginning was rhythm.'"

"And you would not permit the use of the little monitor, even if it brought about the desired result—that is, educated the pupil to a sense of rhythm, which he seemed to lack at the start?"

"No," was the decided answer, "for the reason that it would be an educated, not an inborn, sense.

TEACHER LIKE A PHYSICIAN

"A thoroughly competent teacher will adapt his work to the needs of each pupil who comes to him. He stands in the place of a physician and should be able to administer the correct remedy for every pianistic ill. He has all kinds of hands and various sorts of minds to deal with. A very long hand, with long fingers, can do quite different things from the short-fingered, plump hand. The weak, flabby hands should have special treatment. Then the mentality of one student is so different from every other. Thus, you see, the resourceful teacher must be ready for every emergency; must be able to teach each pupil according to his needs."

RESTORING ONE'S TECHNIC IN FIFTEEN DAYS

"How are you able to keep your large repertoire in review, while maintaining technic at concert pitch?" he was asked.

"I learn easily, and must remember what I have learned. During the war, I was three years without a piano, and therefore did not touch a note. When I was free and could return to the piano, I was able to bring back my facility and repertoire in fifteen days.

"During the three years that I had no opportunity to use a piano, I was determined to keep my fingers, hands and arms flexible in some way. I did many gymnastics with them, inventing all sorts of forms, so that they should keep in good condition. I also had a silent keyboard to work on, and found it a most helpful and wonderful aid to the keeping up of one's technic. It seemed remarkable to me that I could get back my facility so quickly; it must have been the gymnastic work I did, with the help of the clavier, and the constant mental effort in keeping my repertoire in review. I always learn everything very thoroughly, from the start.

A PIECE LEARNED IS A PIECE MEMORIZED

"I consider it absolutely essential for the piano student to commit everything he attempts to learn, to memory. If he wishes to enlarge his acquaintance with music by getting the works of various composers and playing them through, there is certainly no harm in that. But this is very different from attempting to learn the pieces. With this end in view, one must study seriously, analyze the music, see how it is made up, consider its form and tone texture, and what the composer evidently intended to convey through it.

"So many points need to be considered in the interpretation of a composition, aside from technical development and performance. One of these aspects is a consideration of the epoch in which the composer lived. The men of a past age surely felt as deeply, as vividly, as we do today, but they had a different idiom of expression. This was partly due to the instruments of former times, which were small and delicate, with little power or tone quality. The technic of those days was adequate for the instruments, but dramatic power was not considered necessary. Therefore we ought to play the older music in the style, tone quality, and with the psychological meaning it had in its own time and epoch. Modern music needs all the resources of the modern instrument, which is capable of expressing both the power and delicacy, the passion and exaltation, that are now deemed essential. The modern piano is a wonderful instrument, and if we understand and can control it, we can express every emotion of which the soul is capable." *

* "A Glimpse of Alfred Cortot in the Class Room," showing how he conducts a class in repertoire, will be found in the author's book, "What to Play—What to Teach," p. 263 (Theodore Presser, Philadelphia).

IV

VLADIMIR DE PACHMANN

A DISTINCTIVE METHOD OF PIANO PLAYING

IF you were to come in touch with that super-lative pianist and unique personality, Vladimir de Pachmann, you would not soon forget the experience. More than this. If you were per-mitted to sit beside the piano as he played for you, now this beautiful bit or that—just as they came into his mind—you would feel you were getting a very near and intimate view of a many-sided artist. If a music lover, you would enjoy the shifting web of tone colors he wove for you alone. A pianist—you would like to capture, imprison and make your own the secrets of tone and touch he illustrated for your benefit. A teacher—the wonderful technical control would appeal to you, which this wizard of the keyboard possesses in such a marvelous degree.

I had the privilege of spending over an hour with the Russian pianist, on two different occa-sions, shortly after he arrived in America for his last tours. The first afternoon several friends

VLADIMIR DE PACHMANN

were present. He was in rather a gay mood. He had left the steamer but a few hours before, and still felt the throb of the machinery. He was glad to be in our country, where people were so sympathetic to his art, and so on. After a while he brought out one of his most treasured possessions, which he exhibited for our admiration. This was nothing less than a coat which had once belonged to Chopin. It was of mohair of a chocolate brown color, with large collar and long skirt. Some one requested him to put it on. Then the piano was surreptitiously opened, and he was induced, still wearing the coat—which was much too large for him—to seat himself at the keyboard. Almost before he was aware of it he was improvising tiny little stray tone-thoughts. Continually protesting that he could not play that day, that he had not touched a piano for two weeks, he began the D flat Nocturne of Chopin.

It was a memorable performance, or rather it was a poetical inspiration in tones. One felt it was the last word in the interpretation of this exquisite night song. He accompaned the playing with a little by-play of remarks as he went along. "This is Caruso," he said in one place; again, "These tones are sung by Patti." The pairs of intervals toward the close, given to the right hand, he called bells. When it was over, he explained that the beauties we admired were due to a new method of playing which he had discovered about five years ago. What this method is has been subsequently much misunderstood, one writer going so far as to say it consists in holding the wrist stiff and high. Nothing could be farther from the truth. He explained his ideas to me the following afternoon, when I spent another hour with him. Calling me to sit beside him at the piano, he began:

"My Méthode, ah yes, I discovered it five years ago. It was a revelation; it came to me from Heaven. It does not consist of high, stiff wrists; that would be very bad—abominable! You see I move my wrists up and down freely when I play. But my hand and arm I hold quite level, with the outside of the hand on a line with the arm, not turned in or out at the wrist.

"In order to preserve this position of hand and arm in different parts of the keyboard, the use of the fingers, or I should say, the choice of them, must be very carefully considered. I must use special fingering for everything I play. Fingering, anyway, is a very important factor in great playing. Take von Bülow, for instance: he did much for fingering in his editions of Beethoven and Chopin. But I do not feel he has solved all the problems, by any means. He always tried to make things more difficult through constant change of fingers, thereby turning the hand from side to side and twisting the fingers out of shape. I make things easy by using fingers that will not throw the hand out of shape and that will always preserve the correct relation of hand to the arm, of which I have spoken. Yet Bülow was a great man, a most excellent pianist, thinker and philosopher. I say all this for him, though I don't approve of his fingering. I care still less for Klindworth's, for he tried to make things more difficult than they need be, in order to keep all fingers employed.

"Look at this passage from Chopin's Third Impromptu. Here is Bülow's fingering; you see how it throws the hand out of shape? Here is mine, which keeps the hand quiet and in natural position.

"The first benefit of my Méthode to the player is that he can produce a *natural tone,* made without effort. I can play hours and hours without fatigue. I could play the whole twenty-four if I didn't have to eat a little and sleep some. But the pianists of today, especially the younger ones—see with what effort they play, and with what a hard tone! How can they ever make natural tones and play from the heart, when they are punching and beating the piano at the rate they do? Ah, the poor piano! But *my* piano will yield lovely tones because I treat it in the right way. Why not caress it like this? Listen to these little upward passages; how delicate and shadowy! How ethereal they can be made if the heart speaks through them by means of the fingers! And the fingers, doing their part through right adjustment and correct choice, glide up and down the keyboard with little or no effort or exertion.

"Do you think all this is easy? Of course it looks perfectly so—and it is easy, for me. But each of these passages has cost me months of study. Some of them I have played thousands of times. And even yet they do not quite suit me; they can still be improved with more labor, till they become superlatively perfect."

And the artless pianist, simple as a child, listened intently, with head on one side, to the exquisite tones he produced.

"When I made the discovery of my Méthode, I soon found that to play my pieces in the new way they must all be revised and fingered anew. Many passages written for one hand I now use both hands for, thus keeping the hands in a more natural position and making things easier for both."

Mr. de Pachmann illustrated his remarks with various passages, most of them taken from the music of Chopin.

"Some pieces do not lend themselves to such changes as are required by my Méthode, and those I shall not play in my recitals.

"Of Beethoven I shall not give the *Appassionata*, for I know it has been done to extinction; every student brings it out. Neither shall the *Waldstein* appear on my programs. Op. 90 is nice in the First Movement; see how this opening theme can be transfigured by beautiful tone. Is it not heavenly? But the last movement I don't care for, and it's too long, as you say. I shall only put the *Sonata Pathétique* on my programs.

"Of Chopin I shall select only the special and least-known pieces. Not the Polonaise Op. 53 or the Scherzo Op. 31. I can't hear these any more; they are played *ad nauseam*. No, I will choose the Fourth Scherzo and two Polonaises, the small one in C sharp minor and the wonderful one in F sharp minor, Op. 44, one of the greatest compositions ever written on this little planet. It is truly inspired. Then I shall give the little-known Allegro de Concerto and a few other things.

"Brahms' Valses will be heard in one of my

New York recitals. How light and beautiful is
Number One; listen to it! Ah, and I will play it
in tempo, too—no hesitation, no lagging. With
my Méthode I can play it that way. Then hear
Number Six; note the lightness of the skips!
They should ripple and dance like tiny fairies.
Do you remember the run in thirty seconds in
Number 14? You will see I can play it in time.
See, I beat the time with my hands and then play.
Ah, you don't hear it played like that, with such
swiftness, lightness and precision.

"Then there is the music of Godowsky, the
greatest since Brahms. He is a great genius,
Godowsky; such a thinker, contrapuntalist, composer and pianist all in one. I have talked with
him already about my Méthode. When he heard
what it really was he understood at once and ex-
claimed, 'Ah, Pachmann, you have found out
something really fine; in this way one can make
a true, natural tone.'

"What has Godowsky written for the piano?
First, there is a wonderful Sonata in five move-
ments; a great work, finer than Brahms' Op. 5.
It is grander, more majestic than that, and ex-
ceedingly difficult. Then there is the *Walzer-
Masken,* a set of twenty-four pieces—*beautiful!*
I shall play seven of them in my American con-
certs. They are finer than the *Trikatammeron,*

the set of thirty pieces of more recent date—at least *I* think so. These I do not play—nor the Sonata—in public; my Méthode is not adapted to them.

"Yes, I intend to write out my Méthode; it shall be set down in an orderly manner, for the benefit of those who come after me. But not yet —I have no time; I must go on tour. After all that is over—then—perhaps——"

After two very successful seasons of concertizing in America, separated by a summer of rest and quiet, the venerable musician decided he must return to his European home. New York had the opportunity to hear him once more before he departed, in a last recital which was called "A farewell for all time."

The last view of a renowned artist—the last time one comes under the spell of his particular form of art—is always memorable. The last American recital of de Pachmann makes history. At least once before he had seemed to take final leave of us, notably in 1912. But the very last "for all time" occurred April 13, 1925.

Many years lay between his early recitals here and the very last of all. Some of us recall the days when he used to play in old Chickering Hall, Fifth Avenue and Eighteenth Street.

Many other artists played there in those days, including von Bülow, Carreno and Scharwenka.

Pachmann was ever erratic and talkative during recital, even in those days. On one occasion, during a long composition, his thought wandered, perhaps from too many side remarks, and he seemed suddenly to have a lapse of memory—or was it a cramp of the wrist, as he indicated it was; we could not quite tell which. He sprang from the chair, clasping his wrist, as though the next moment the hand would drop off, all the time talking very fast.

Pacing up and down the platform, still holding his wrist, he slowly indicated that he was recovering the use of his hand. He then went to the piano, made several attempts to use his fingers, and finally told us he would try to continue the composition. He began the interrupted piece at the beginning, and this time went through it in safety.

At the *really* farewell recital, Carnegie Hall was quite filled, and several hundred were seated on the stage. We all waited as patiently as we might, till long past the hour, remembering it was the last time. Finally a small figure threaded its way to the front of the stage, smiling, bowing, and talking as it came. When the piano was reached, the piano-stool proved to be intractable, and an orderly was summoned to adjust it. Meanwhile the eccentric pianist explained to the audience that the fingers and wrist of his right hand were troubling him; it was strenuous business to play a whole recital, at his age, too. He might get through all right; if he did, it would all be due to his wonderful Méthode and Heaven's blessing on his work.

With many glances Heavenward and at the audience, he seated himself before the instrument. It was an "all Chopin" program, and even the severest critics concede that de Pachmann, at his best, can be inimitable in the smaller Chopin pieces. For the greater Chopin he never had, even in his prime, sufficient virility and power. And on this final occasion the strength of former days was lacking. But there were compensations—unforgettable moments, when we listened almost breathless to the fine-spun, gossamer delicacy of the F major Étude, or to the ethereal loveliness of the D flat Nocturne. Some of the shorter Valses and Mazurkas were equally enthralling. Together these blossoms of delicate memory formed a nosegay of rarest fragrance, whose aroma is a lasting memory.

Let us close eyes and ears to those eccentric grimaces and the running fire of comment; for both these are distracting whenever we allow them to divert our attention. But let us rather treasure the remembrance of the few but exquisite tone pictures which Vladimir de Pachmann has left us as a rich legacy.

V

IGNAZ FRIEDMAN

SELF-DEVELOPMENT A NECESSITY FOR THE PIANIST

"You must hear Ignaz Friedman, pianist and composer; for me he is the greatest piano virtuoso," remarked another piano virtuoso, also great, recently to the writer.

"In what way is he the greatest?" was asked.

"In poetic conception especially, though he also has a marvelous technic; indeed he is unique among pianists."

What first impresses in the playing of Friedman, is the intensity of his musical utterance, the poetical imagination, the sense of tone color, raised to its highest emotional power. Later on we begin to realize Friedman possesses a formidable technic, capable of expressing and revealing an intensely artistic temperament, in many and diverse moods.

Piano technic may be acquired with industry and perseverance. When acquired, it can only reflect the individuality of the performer possessing it. The pianist of frigid temperament will reveal himself in a technic corresponding to that temperament. His playing will lack the divine spark, though he may have consummate command of his instrument. The musician of ardent, poetical nature, saturated with poetry and the lyric spirit, will reveal in his technic the qualities peculiar to himself. His playing will be living, vital, and will make an instant appeal. Thus it may be said that artistic technic is not an exterior circumstance, which any one may acquire with sufficient labor, but is in itself an art and provides the means for unfolding the inner life of the artist in all its eloquence.

This idea is aptly illustrated in the piano playing of Ignaz Friedman. With him it is impossible to separate technic from temperament, for they together form a complete musical personality. His technic is nobly expressive of both the greatest delicacy and orchestral power and sonority. Indeed, Friedman rightly deserves the title, Interpreter. For interpretation does not merely signify the slavish mechanical reproduction of a composition, nor is it the capricious disfigurement of the composer's thought, to suit the whim of the player. No, it is something much more noble and sincere. It has been said that the most lovely colors in a score are not those

IGNAZ FRIEDMAN

written down in notes. Nor can words express,
in any language, the living meanings of music.
For there is much in music which escapes sign or
word. The imagination of the artist must pene-
trate far deeper than these indications given by
the composer, must seize and divulge the true
spirit of the work.

If the feeling for rhythm and accent indicate
a vigorous musical mentality, the poetic use of
rubato—as in Chopin—proves the possession of
an imaginative, flexible temperament, which pre-
serves the inner rhythm of the music, while expressing every shade of emotion.

When speaking of Friedman the Pole, one
instinctively thinks of Chopin the Pole; not because the former fails to interpret other masters,
but simply because he seems especially adapted
to the music of Chopin.

In the works of Chopin, as in those of all sincere composers, may be traced personal characteristics. Chopin, the delicately organized,
dreamer of dreams, was keenly alive to patriot-
ism—a complex, intense nature. This conception of Chopin is divined by Friedman, with a
sympathy almost amounting to genius.

If Chopin was one of the greatest geniuses of
the piano, preceding modern French, Russian
and Spanish composers, the other foundations

of piano literature rest in Beethoven, Schumann and Liszt. Friedman, in rendering the works of these masters, deserves the title of super-virtuoso of the piano. He reproduces in Beethoven the rhythmic and melodic beauty, the grandeur of classic outlines, as in Sonatas 57 and 111. In Schumann, the profound poesy and lyricism found in the Carneval and Symphonic Études; in Liszt the dizzy heights of dazzling bravura.

The pianistic interpretation of Beethoven has occupied recondite virtuosos and musical philosophers for many a year, each in his own way. From Bülow to Risler, to mention two extremes, the pianists who have devoted themselves to the Master of Bonn, have presented him in the most diverse lights. For Beethoven reveals himself to each mentality in a different way. His art is not like a piece of granite, always the same. Rather is it an aggregate mass of glowing life. Musical art does not become immobile in order to assume one unique aspect, as in painting and sculpture; it is rather the incessant reproduction of forms and ideas.

Friedman presents Beethoven at once as a classicist and romanticist—as form and spirit. Standing as he did at the confluence of two epochs, Beethoven did not cast aside classical material. The spirit of Beethoven, influenced by the parallel which exists between literature and music, glimpsed a romantic world, a world of freedom and independence of thought in music. Yet he remained on the threshold of this new world, not yet entering into its full presence. Beethoven appears to us a romanticist still under the partial influence of classicism.

"To our mind," asserts an excellent musical authority, "this is the manner in which Friedman understands Beethoven. The Polish pianist knows how to express the ardent but new-born romanticism of Beethoven within the symmetrical form of classicism, mingling grace and delicacy with exaltation and ardor—the very soul of romanticism."

After these thoughts on the art of Friedman the artist and musician, let us approach Friedman the man.

In many little, unexpected ways, Ignaz Friedman is unique and individual. For instance: on arriving in America, instead of going at once to one of the great hotels of New York—to some popular hostelry, where he would see the gilt-edged side of the city's life, which eddies about Thirty-fourth or Forty-second Streets—he chose to locate in one on lower Fifth Avenue, which, to be sure, is much nearer the heart of old New

York. A short distance away, Paderewski's "Washington Arch" rises above the square, while many little streets lead off into unexpected quaintnesses.

As one approaches the spot through a couple of these old streets, one finds here and there fascinating little shops, filled with wares from many parts of the world. Rare porcelains and bronzes peep out at you from basement windows; quaint signs on doorways invite you to enter and purchase. Odd eating-places along the way tempt you to try them, just to see what they are like. Some other time we will come this way and explore, but not today. For just now we are bound for the hotel where is to be found Ignaz Friedman, the astonishing pianist.

"Yes, Mr. Friedman will see you at once," was the response to our question. And we were scarcely seated in the comfortable little parlor, when the pianist entered with cordial greeting.

A man of kindly and simple manners, inclined to be reserved, yet ready to respond to a sincere desire to know his views on musical subjects, especially on piano study. By way of introduction, he was asked how he happened to locate so far from the city's fashionable center.

"I like it here, it suits me. I would not feel comfortable in a fashionable place; then, too, this is more European. When I walk about in this vicinity, I feel as if I were on the other side of the globe. Yes, I can practise here, all I wish. I have a dumb piano, too, how do you call it—a 'practice clavier'? It may be a Virgil Clavier; it is an American instrument, anyway; I always have it with me."

"It is good to know you approve working on such a mental instrument as the practice clavier," we remarked.

"Oh, yes, indeed, I approve of it. One must do much technical practise each day, if one would not have one's mechanism become rusty. The pianist must have a big technic, in these days of great technical achievements. He must have much more technic than he really needs for the works he plays. Ten times more, you ask? Yes, that is about the proportion. When he possesses such an equipment, then piano playing is an easy matter, for then he has perfect control of himself and his instrument.

"And now as to some of the most important technical principles used in piano playing. Perhaps the first is

CONSERVATION OF ENERGY

"Learn to reserve your strength. Do not put out any more strength, power or vital force than you absolutely need. Then you do not become so fatigued by much practise or playing.

NO SHORT-CUT TO PIANO MASTERY

"I have made myself familiar with the whole literature for the mastering of piano technic. One must do so if one would know whatever has been accomplished along this line. I assure you, at the outset, there is positively no short-cut to the mastering of the piano. If any one affirms there is, he says what is false. Students think if they play a dozen études of Czerny, they have acquired all he has said; but they have not. There is a great deal more to Czerny than that. It is the same with many other technical masters who have contributed to the literature for acquiring mechanical perfection.

"When one has worked through all the important material of this nature, it is only the outside shell after all. It is the proper assimilation of all this material which will adequately equip the artist; it is what he makes out of it; it is what the artist does for himself. No one can do this for him; no teacher, no set of études, no mass of finger gymnastics. It is self-instruction—self-development.

PRINCIPLES

"To go back to our enumeration of foundation principles. They can be given in a single sentence. The hand must be arched at the knuckles, the fingers firm at the nail joint, the wrist loose. Clear, articulate finger action is necessary. Arm weight must be under control, so that too much is not allowed to rest on the fingers in passage playing; otherwise a heavy tone is produced, and the player becomes sooner wearied."

Observers of Mr. Friedman's playing have noticed the absolute freedom from effort with which he plays. This consummate ease is doubtless one of his artistic secrets.

THE PEDALS

"The pedals, too, have a special technic of their own. Sometimes the pedal is taken *before,* sometimes *with,* and frequently *after* the note or chord. Often a fine effect is made by omitting the pedal altogether. The understanding of when and how to use these various effects comes only through a close analysis of the piece, its harmonic structure and the artistic effect which should be produced.

MEMORIZING

"How do I memorize?" The artist smiled, as though the subject were either too large or too inconsequent to mention. Then he said:

"One must know the piece, its construction and harmony, through careful study. There are four sources of memory: the eye, to see the notes on the page or keys—that would be visual memory; the fingers, to find the keys easily on the keyboard—digital memory; the ear, to hear the tones —auricular memory; and, lastly, though we might say it should be first, the mind to think these tones and keys—or mental memory.

"In the case of young students, they should learn the principal chords of the keys—tonic, dominant and dominant seventh—with their different positions. All these can be found in the simple pieces they are studying. And they ought to analyze the chords and learn how the melodies are formed from them In this way they discover how the piece is put together, and can better memorize and retain it.

THE TRILL

"About the best exercise and most useful one, is the trill. It can be employed by each pair of fingers in turn; that is to say, with 1-2, 2-3, 3-4,

4-5. It can be beneficially used by pairing off other fingers, such as 1-3, 1-4, or 1-4, 2-3. The trill gives facility and control to the fingers and should always be kept up.

APPLYING TECHNIC TO PIECES

"In piano playing it is experience that counts for so much. Even if you acquire a good technic, it is not of much use unless you employ those principles in the pieces you study. And so, in the constant effort to do this, experience is gained, also that fine sense of balance and proportion, without which artistic performance is not possible. All this takes time—much time. I began to play the piano when I was three, and have been at it ever since—thirty odd years; I surely should know whereof I speak. Indeed, in all these years I should have learned what there is to learn and know about piano playing.

THE HAND OF A PIANIST

"The formation of the hand of a pianist is a very important part of his equipment; therefore this should be a paramount consideration. The first question is, has he a hand that will reward cultivation? Some persons love music, but are not physically fitted to become pianists; they would be more at home with 'cello or violin. My hand now," holding up and regarding his own perfectly formed and developed member, "is really fitted to play the piano; I could not handle the violin with any success."

As Ignaz Friedman has related, he began to attempt the piano at the tender age of three; at eight he played exceedingly well, and his musicianship was such that he could transpose Bach's Preludes and Fugues without difficulty. He was at that time a piano prodigy and toured Poland, Russia and the Continent. Later he settled down to very serious study, went to Vienna and remained with Leschetizky for a number of years, finally becoming his assistant.

As a composer, Friedman has almost a hundred compositions to his credit, including a piano concerto, a quintette for piano and strings, three string quartettes, piano pieces and songs.

Further proof of his musicianship is found in his work of editing the entire Chopin and Liszt publications. He is now at work on similar editions of Bach and Schumann.

VI

ALEXANDER BRAILOWSKY

THOUGHT AND FEELING IN PIANO PLAYING

It was in a season more or less dominated by Russians, especially Russian pianists, that I first heard Alexander Brailowsky. November was at least half over; Medtner had just been heard in recital and with orchestra. The later arrival, younger and less known, had not yet made his début. Under such circumstances, artists are generally loath to be questioned. But Mr. Brailowsky was most considerate, and, together with his charming wife, we had a very pleasant and intimate chat.

EARLY STUDIES

"I scarcely know just when I began to play the piano; playing, from the start, seemed to come natural to me. Even technic itself was made a childhood pastime for me. My father, a musical amateur of fine taste and cultivation, played the piano well. He showed me the first steps and helped me over the early stages. I can remember, when I was only five, how my father and I used to sit at the piano and play scales together, each of us trying to see which one would get to the top of the keyboard first! What fun we had with those scales! I would try to beat Father in speed and accuracy, but he was usually a little ahead. It was splendid drill for me, though, and I believe such early practise of scales is invaluable for any child who has real musical ability.

"Later on, as it seemed music was to be my lifework, I was sent to a large music school in Kiev, the city of my birth, to begin the serious study of music. I was about eight years old at the time. My teacher at this school was Pouchalsky, a former pupil of Leschetizky. After several years of earnest study in my home city, I went to Vienna and put myself into the hands of Leschetizky. I therefore feel that I have, all my life, been under the influence of this great master and teacher. I remained with him for more than three years, that is to say, from 1911 to the year the World War began.

"When I went to this master, he seemed pleased with the technic I had so far acquired, for I had been developing it for years. However, I went to one of his assistants for a time, to see that everything was as he would like to have it.

For Miss Brower
as a friendly
remembrance of
A. Brailowsky.
New York
Nov. 23rd 1925

ALEXANDER BRAILOWSKY

"During all my musical studies, from the very beginning, I was never trained to consider the mechanical side of piano playing of supreme and overwhelming importance. I was never made to raise my fingers to just a certain height, nor employed the so-called hammer-touch. Neither was I trained to hold the hand after a certain pattern. Leschetizky always said he had no set method himself; he left that side of the work to his assistants, and each one of these had a little different manner of presenting technical ideas and principles. He also said that, as each student who came to him was of a different caliber and mentality, he must necessarily teach each one differently. He desired to create artistic and musical individuality in each student. In my case, we naturally worked on the interpretative side, as illustrated in the compositions of Beethoven, Schumann, Chopin and Liszt."

TECHNICAL PRACTISE

Replying to the question of what material for technic practise, and whether he used mechanical forms of pure technic, outside of pieces, the pianist answered in the negative.

"No, I do not use abstract forms—indeed, I have never done so. There is plenty of technical material to be found in pieces, if one is willing to get right to work and master the knotty problems which occur in any large, serious work. Indeed, I cannot always tell—or put into words—just how I shall go to work to master a passage or piece; the mastery seems to come to me of itself. Again, I do not know, to a nicety, just how I shall interpret a composition after I have made it my own. I have no cut-and-dried manner of playing it; if I had, there would be no opportunity for the inspiration of the moment. When I am alone, communing with my piano, poetic fantasy often carries me away, and I play quite differently from what I do before an audience, where everything must be more circumspect and exact. My wife will bear me out in this statement."

"It is quite true," replied Madame. "He plays very differently when he is alone, or for me—I sometimes scarcely recognize his playing in concert."

INSPIRED BY AN AUDIENCE

"As I said, I cannot tell, beforehand, exactly how I shall play a certain composition at a given time. I am not one who believes a piece must always be played in just one certain way; that having thought out a conception, the player must always slavishly adhere to it. For in this way there would be no room for spontaneous feeling, for emotion or inspiration. Keeping the general trend and idea of the piece before the mind, I must have some chance to play as I feel.

"An audience can have great effect on the sensibilities of an artist. I can feel at once if any of my listeners are sympathetic, if they are with me and appreciate what I am doing. This mentality in the audience is a tremendous help to an artist and urges him to do his best. A cold or unsympathetic audience has, naturally, the opposite effect, and no one is so quick to sense this atmosphere as the player himself.

AMOUNT OF PRACTISE

"I do not practise so very much, only about five hours a day; but, as you say, one can do a great deal in that time, with complete concentration. Of course, situated as we are, in a hotel, I can only do an hour or so, and must go out to get the rest of the time at the piano. But one can do much study away from the instrument, in thinking—*thinking* the music; indeed, it is *all* thinking, in reality. Leschetizky's principle was to do much practise away from the piano. For many reasons this is a necessity.

REPERTOIRE

"Of course I play the classics, but am especially partial to romantic music, Schumann and Chopin. I consider Chopin the greatest composer for the piano. I can say, with truth, that I am not only familiar with all that Chopin ever wrote, but that I play all his music. It is hardly necessary to add that I love this music more than the music of any other composer. It has more poetry, more idealism—at least for me. In Paris, before I left, I gave six programs of his music—I might add, to sold-out houses, showing that French people love his music also. On my piano you will notice a rare portrait of Chopin——" pointing to a picture in color. "It represents a likeness of the Polish master when excited or inspired in playing his own music. It is a copy of a painting by de la Croix, and was presented to me by Pleyel in Paris. One of the six programs I mentioned—one given last April —contained both the Concertos, the Andante Spianato and Polonaise, Op. 22; the Variations on Mozart's 'La ci darem la mano,' Op. 2; the Grande Fantaisie on Polish Airs, Op. 13, and La Krakowiak, Op. 14.

"Yes, most certainly there is a special technic needed to play Chopin's music. It should always be very fluent, fluid, delicate, airy and capable of great variety of color. For this reason the player who would interpret Chopin's music most artistically, should choose a piano with a very facile action and not too deep a touch. I use a Pleyel in Paris and wherever I can get it, as that responds to the lightest pressure.

"As to the program for my début in America, it is one I have used in many countries. It begins and ends with Liszt. I shall start with the Liszt B minor Sonata, which is a great favorite of mine, and I look forward to playing it in America. This Sonata seems to me one of the greatest works ever written for the piano; it is a true masterpiece. I have heard it played by many artists, and each one finds something individual in it and different from others. Each reading, from Paderewski's down, is interesting, for such a great romantic work is susceptible of great variety of treatment.

"Yes, I play much modern music also. We have various composers in Russia today who are doing good work, each in his own manner, in his own sphere of thought. A few have come to live among you, like Rachmaninoff and Siloti, also Godowsky. Others visit you—Medtner, Prokofieff, Stravinsky, Skriabin. I shall play some Moussorgsky pieces on my first program. We all bring of our art to you, feeling assured of your sympathy and your appreciation."

With his tall, slender figure bowed over the keyboard—as though he loved it—Brailowsky sits as though entranced by the music he evolves, as though utterly oblivious to the listeners who sit before him as under a spell. The tones he produces are always luscious in quality, whether they are of feathery lightness or of splendid sonority. Never once are they harsh or strident. Everything he does has the stamp of a poetic individuality. No matter how hackneyed the piece, he seems to create it anew and hold it up in a fresh light—as he did the Chopin A flat Ballade, the D flat Valse and the Nocturne in E flat. These effects he produces by wonderful tone coloring, by varied nuance, by dwelling ever so slightly on a note here and there, by accents and exceptionally artistic control of the pedals. With him the pedal is truly "the soul of the piano." The Liszt B minor Sonata, under his fingers, becomes heroic, tender, appealing, triumphant. He brings out the gentler side at times where others see the bombastic and self-important. Yet there is plenty of power where it is needed. He has indeed a touch "ravishing in the range and character of its expressive dynamics," as one writer expressed it.

One might almost say the caliber of an artist is shown by the character of the encores he grants. Those given by this artist were always dignified, though some were worn threadbare. That made no difference. The listener might feel he had never heard the E flat Nocturne before, it was so tenderly soulful, without being in the least sentimental. Did the Mendelssohn *Spinning Song* ever ripple and scintillate more beautifully? Or the *Traumeswirren* of Schumann ever sound so clear and simple, so delicate? As a parting gift came La Campanella, tossed off with astonishing bravura.

It was all enthralling piano playing, from which the student, the young pianist and the teacher could learn much of tone coloring, power and lightness, of accent and rhythmic security, of poetic feeling and true artistic inspiration.

VII

WALTER GIESEKING

RELAXATION A PRIME ESSENTIAL

A NEW star in the pianistic firmament!
Walter Gieseking has been called a musical
genius and a pianistic phenomenon at the same
time. Also it is said he has the ability, the power,
to project the thought and meaning of the music
he plays, so that it at once appeals to the listener.
Indeed, the critics of Europe have showered un-
stinted praise upon him, and after his first
appearances in America, the most glowing trib-
utes were chronicled.

After hearing the new pianist on each occasion, always with the desire to form an unbiased
opinion, it seemed to this listener that he has
indeed a very beautiful pianistic mechanism. His
arms and hands, from shoulder to finger-tips,
seem to be completely relaxed, so that his legato
passage playing is smooth as oil, and his manipu-
lation of the keyboard appears to be absolutely
effortless. His Bach and Mozart are delicately
clear, with each tiny shade and nuance in its

appropriate place. His Debussy is all in cool, pastel shades, subtly impersonal. He seems very fond of the most airy qualities of tone color and indulges in these shimmering half-lights and shadows to such an extent that we cannot help wishing, at times, for some rich, vibrant tones by way of contrast. Still, the twilight tints are very alluring and incite to dreams. The pianist enters heart and soul into everything he plays, and while his fingers glide over the keys in this effortless fashion, his head and body reflect the intensity of his thought—especially in rapid passages—by many jerks and movements.

We will let Mr. Gieseking relate, in a few words, some incidents of his musical career, as he told them to me, sitting near his piano, in his hotel suite.

"I was born in Lyons, France, in 1895. My father was a physician and had a post in Italy. So I spent my first sixteen years on the Italian Riviera. I was, from a tiny chap, very fond of music, and picked up my piano playing somehow by myself. I read and played everything I could lay hands on. It was not till we went to Hanover, Germany, to live, in 1911—when I was sixteen—that I really began to study music seriously. I entered the Hanover Conservatory, where I had Karl Leimer for a teacher.

"I was with him three years—then came the war, which put an end, for the time being, to many things I had planned to do, though of course I kept right on with my studies. Leimer was my only teacher, as I never had any other. After these three years with him, I decided to make music my profession and began gradually to appear in recital. I progressed in this line of effort until now, each season, I have more than one hundred concerts to play, so that I have little time for anything else.

MEMORY STUDY

"To commit to memory is a very simple matter with me, unless the composition happens to be very difficult. A great deal can be accomplished by reading the music through away from the piano. As I read it the eye takes in the characters on the printed page while the ear hears them mentally. After a few times reading through, I often know the piece, can go to the piano and play it from memory. Take this Concerto of Mozart"—picking up a small 12mo score from the table. "This is simple, so far as notes go, and can be learned in the way I speak of. But the Hindemith Concerto, here, which I played with the New York Symphony Orchestra, is much more difficult. I read this through also, but in small sections—line by line. Afterward I must play it often, too, to fix it in memory. As you see," showing me the music, "it has many uneven and irregular rhythms. We had four rehearsals with orchestra, before the concert, as it was the first performance in America."

HAND POSITION

If you speak to Gieseking about normal hand position at the piano, he is mystified, for all positions are equally admissible to him, depending on the requirements of the music. Sometimes his hand is high and arched, then it is flat, with wrist dropped far below the keyboard. "I have a good hand for the piano," he says, as he holds it up; "and the fingers are flexible, as you see."—which he proved by bending them far back, at right-angles with the back of the hand. It is indeed a wonderful hand, and must resemble Rubinstein's. Indeed, Gieseking has been called the German Rubinstein.

AMOUNT OF PRACTISE

"I really need very little practise," continued the pianist, "as I do not forget what I have learned; my fingers don't forget either. In the summer I take a couple of months off for rest and recreation, and often do not touch a piano or even see one, in all that time. But this seems to make no difference with my playing. After the vacation I can return and at once give a recital or play with orchestra without the least difficulty. All of which proves I do not need much visible practise. During my concert season, of course, I have little time for practise, but I can study new works, on trains, as I travel about.

TECHNICAL MATERIAL

"With technical forms, pure and simple, I have done comparatively little. There is the C major scale, for instance. Its construction is very simple, and this form can be applied to all other scales or keys. The C scale, however, seems to me the most difficult of all, on account of the wider crossing of hand over thumb. As you notice, B, E or others are easier." Mr. Gieseking demonstrated various scale forms, running them up and down the keyboard with amazing swiftness. "Then, after scales come accords—arpeggios or broken chords. These formed from chord positions are simple, too. These few things my teacher required. After these I was given études. I *think* it was the Cramer Studies I had to learn. And after these came the Clementi *Gradus,* and later I worked on the Chopin Études, as every pianist must."

REPERTOIRE

Asked about his repertoire, the artist took several sheets of notepaper from the table: "These are the pieces I play," he said simply. A rapid glance revealed some of the larger Bach compositions, as well as a group of Preludes and Fugues. Numerous Sonatas of Beethoven came next.

"Of course I know all the Beethoven Sonatas, but from those indicated I will choose for my present concerts. As you see, I have the Schubert *Wanderer Fantaisie,* Op. 15, of which I am very fond, besides other compositions of this master. Then some Schumann and much Debussy. Both books of Preludes—twelve numbers each—besides other pieces of the French composer. You doubtless notice an absence of Chopin. I do not play his music, though I know it, of course. But I have refrained from using it to any extent in my recitals, for it is overplayed. Almost every program of every pianist has a group of this music; sometimes it is an 'all-Chopin program.' So I want to give other things, that are not so very familiar.

"Do I play American music—MacDowell? I do not know American music—yet; though I am slightly acquainted with some of your Mac-Dowell's shorter pieces—not the Sonatas. Ah, yes, the *Hexen Tanz,* that is a charming composition," and turning to the piano he played it in part, with the fleetness and delicacy for which he is so noted.

PLAYING WITH ORCHESTRA

"In playing with orchestra, the quality of tone of the two instruments should blend artistically. If one pianist's scale of dynamics is less boisterous and militant than another, the orchestra should adapt itself to the reduced scale of the soloist. For my part, I feel that the whole conception of performance in these days is too heavy, loud and blatant. I prefer less power, but, instead, more delicacy and ethereal refinement of tone."

In his two New York recitals, Gieseking has chosen compositions with which he feels a peculiar affinity. Of Bach a Partita and the English Suite No. 6 in D minor. Then the Schubert *Wanderer* and Schumann's *Kreislerianna,* and finally Debussy's Twenty-four Preludes, equally divided between each list. This music does not make much noise. It is introspective, intimate, refined, poetical. And the choice of it and the interpretation of it reveal the qualities of this master pianist.

VIII

JOSEF LHEVINNE

THE ART OF MODERN PIANISM

ONE of the most eminent of modern Russian pianists is Josef Lhevinne. Mr. Lhevinne toured this country "before the war," and expected to return here in a year or two to repeat his successes. But the world conflict prevented him from leaving Germany. This state of things was a keen disappointment to the pianist, as a second tour had already been planned. At last the enforced ban was lifted, and he was able to return to the United States, where he now resides.

His success was phenomenal. Those who were a bit curious to know how time had dealt with this artist, or whether he would return as great as he seemed on his first visit, need have had no fear. He was equal to his former self and even better. For, to the limpid clearness of his touch, to the great dynamic range of color, to the extremes of power and delicacy and velocity, he

Photo. *George Maillard Kesslere, B. P.*

JOSEF LHEVINNE

added a deeper note, a more subtle expressiveness, a more sympathetic, soulful quality.

After a long season filled with concerts, he gave six weeks of his summer to the work of teaching, all day—day in and day out—at a summer school.

It was Josef Lhevinne the artist-teacher with whom I wished to confer when he came to my studio the other afternoon. Lhevinne the brilliant virtuoso is known the world over; but the artist-teacher is only known to a comparatively few. It should be at once set down that Mr. Lhevinne has a winning personality. He is most kind in his effort to answer the inquirer, carefully choosing words that will most clearly express his ideas.

PIANO TOUCH

"Touch is indeed the greatest desideratum," he said. "How you touch the piano determines the kind of tones you produce. Touch is the thing that all players work most for. There are the fundamental touches—legato, non-legato, staccato, and sharp staccato. I consider the legato touch most difficult of them all. The tones produced by each finger must connect perfectly; in fact, they may sometimes overlap just a hair's-breadth, in order to sound perfectly legato to the ear. If you say legato can be made with pedal just as well as with fingers, I answer it may be possible to do this, and different effects can be made in this way, but they have not the same quality as though connected by the fingers. For the purest legato is that made with the fingers alone.

TONE IN PIANO PLAYING

"Tone in piano playing is the result of touch. Therefore, I repeat, the way you touch the piano keys determines the kind of tones you produce from them. Yet we do not forget that the piano is a mechanical instrument, and the mere depressing of a key can be done by any one, whether he be a musician or not.

"There must be certain ways of conquering this seemingly mechanical instrument, and turning it into a medium for varied and artistic expression. For, since there seems to be no science or art in merely putting the keys down, there must be many other things to be considered when studying how to produce an expressive tone. If, as some maintain, the piano is simply a mechanical instrument, why is it that from this mechanical medium one player will produce only sharp, strident tones, while another will bring forth tones of melting sweetness and beauty?

"A broad answer might be, because one player has only the idea of sharp sounds in his mind, while the other has a mental concept of sounds of artistic beauty. We know the piano is capable, under certain conditions, of answering to both concepts. Therefore it is, in the last analysis, the mentality of the performer that brings out the quality he seeks, provided he has the ability to realize his ideal.

FINGER ACTION

"As a foundation for every touch stands the one produced by well-developed finger action. All players must acquire this—the sooner the better. *Fingers must be raised.* Nothing else so develops clearness of touch, trains the muscles and forms the background for good technic. Just how much the hand must be arched to produce this touch depends greatly on the formation of the hand. Very long fingers are apt to develop a metallic tone if held too rounded. This much at least can be said: rounded fingers played on the tips produce a more or less brilliant tone; fingers played more upon the ball produce a more velvety quality. For some very delicate effects fingers are held quite close to the keys and scarcely raised at all. So we discover we need two kinds of position and touch, diametrically opposed to each other, namely: *high finger action* and *low action,* with fingers held close to the keys. Every pianist must have both these.

HAND FIRMNESS NECESSARY

"There must be hand firmness, or there is no power, exactness or control. There must be finger firmness also, or there is no accuracy, and consequently no good tone.

"Then, it may be asked, where does relaxation come in? Principally in the wrist and arm. The secret of its use and application is to use it in the right place, and not in other places where it would prevent the production of firm, elastic, vibrant tone. That kind of tone is not produced by flabby, relaxed fingers. We must have both firmness and relaxation at one and the same time, *but not in the same place.* There must generally be resistance in the fingers, no matter how loose wrists and arms may be.

"This seeming contradiction of terms is one of the difficulties of touch and tone production, and the subject should be early understood. We can recall some pianists now before the public who are so excessively relaxed that there is much to be desired in the way of accuracy and clearness in their playing. There are others who go to the other extreme and are stiff and tense, producing a hard, metallic tone.   The golden mean is a just mingling of both principles.

WEIGHT TOUCH

"There must always be some weight, even if one plays the veriest pianissimo, or *ppp*.   Without weight the tone sounds thin and dry.   Just as a voice without resonance has no carrying power, so touch without any weight has no quality.   To learn how to graduate this use of weight to suit the various effects desired is a great study.   No one can tell the player just how to do this; he must learn it—must find it out himself, by experiments.   It comes after one is thoroughly grounded in the fundamentals, not before.   Little can be done with effects until the foundation is thoroughly laid.

LACK OF FUNDAMENTALS

"Among the fundamental things pupils generally lack are rhythmic precision, variety of tone color, principles of relaxation, and the like. A student should have a good understanding and thorough working knowledge of all these.   How is it that Americans, as a rule, need so much help in the matter of time beating and counting? You don't seem to be a very rhythmic people. Therefore there must be extra time and care expended on this side of the musical education. Sometimes, of course, the irregular time counts are the result of nervousness. The player who lacks repose, fails to hold out the tone or beat, owing to nervous haste. It requires a healthy body and calm nerves to play the piano correctly. In the early stages much counting and time beating must be gone through. One can at least acquire a mechanical rhythm with hard work, yet he who has a natural, innate sense of rhythm should consider himself fortunate. But then, all in all, it takes hard work to master the piano, for it is a very difficult instrument, perhaps the most difficult of all.

THE PIANO

"For me the piano is the most perfect instrument, outside the orchestra. Even the string quartet, considered by musicians such an ideal combination, does not equal the piano—to my mind—as a medium of expression. That this opinion has been shared by many of the greatest composers, is proved by the rich literature they have provided for the piano. It exceeds in greatness that of all other instruments combined. Even the human voice, which can be so soulful, requires words to make it understood. But some emotions, like sorrow, tragedy, despair, exaltation, are too deep for words: language cannot express them. Then we must turn to the piano, upon which we can voice our inmost soul in the language of tones without words.

"I referred just now to the things pupils generally lack. Most of all it is a lack of foundation. The young people here in America are not willing to study seriously; they seem to have no desire to lay a thorough foundation, unless they aspire to become artists. For this cause they will work—yes—because they have a financial end in view. But to understand the foundation, no, they do not care. They only want to do a little frivolous learning. In this respect we are so much more thorough in Russia. Students are obliged to go through a certain course of training in the schools and conservatories. They must spend several years in technical training and pass examinations on it. The teachers, too, must pass their examinations and secure a certificate, otherwise they cannot teach. You will need to have certificated teachers here in America, if you expect to have thorough work done.

INSPIRATION BEFORE AN AUDIENCE

"One cannot always be in exalted mood, either when alone or before an audience. In the latter case, it is a very comfortable feeling when one is quite able to forget the audience—to be oblivious to what is on the other side of the footlights. Then one need only think of what the music expresses, and try to voice its meaning. Sometimes it is a picture which is suggested to one's mind, it may be a sad one, or, if the music be gay, one can think of some animated scene—with flowers, lights, the dance, beautiful women and the like. Or it may be a mood that takes possession of the player. Then the mind wanders at will, or without, with no definite picture in view. Of course the player, to be able to be swayed by these pictures or moods, must possess a technic which controls his mechanism and the instrument; in other words, he must have control over himself. This is why the artist is continually working on his technic. He is in duty bound to do so, otherwise his muscles become flabby and do not obey the will.

CONCERT HALL OR STUDIO

"Do I play the same in a small room as in a large hall? I have often considered this question, and have decided that I do play with the same quality and power of tone; that I have not two styles, one for the large and one for the small space. If the artist has clearness and variety of tone and touch, they ought to carry equally in a large hall, without extra effort. Even pianissimo effects, if properly produced, should be heard to the farthest corner of a large auditorium. Yes, *if* properly produced—that is to say, if weight touch is used, so that the tone has resonance and is not a dead tone.

A FINAL WORD ON RELAXATION

"One of the most important, as well as one of the most practical, things to be acquired by the pianist is a knowledge of the principle of relaxation and how it may be applied to touch and tone. When one speaks of relaxation one meets with many obstacles, so little is the correct use of relaxation understood. Everything that 'flops' is called by this name when it may be very wide of the mark and mean nothing at all. The whole world has gone mad over the idea of relaxation, without knowing what it means, or how it should be applied to piano playing. From what I have already said you see one must combine the two principles of firmness and relaxation, at the same time but not in the same place. The application of these principles to obtain varied effects forms one of the most fascinating studies in the Art of Modern Pianism."

A few words should be added in behalf of

Mme. Rosina Lhevinne, who in some ways is the equal of her gifted husband. As a pianist she possesses a technic very similar to his, in tone quality, variety and fleetness. The ensemble playing of these pianists is as near perfection as seems humanly possible to achieve. Mme. Lhevinne is also an excellent teacher, of great assistance to her husband in this direction.

IX

WANDA LANDOWSKA

THE CHARMS OF OLD MUSIC

WANDA LANDOWSKA, patron saint of the harpsichord and its wealth of rare old music, is herself a charming personality. To come in touch with her is like meeting with a musician from the time of Bach and Scarlatti, who in some mysterious fashion appears to belong to the present, though revealing the spirit of the past.

As one enters her artistic studios high up in one of New York's residential hotels, situated in the heart of the city, one comes upon a beautiful harpsichord, made by Pleyel of Paris especially for this unique artist. A little farther away stands a modern grand piano. It is pleasant to imagine her at work on one instrument or on the other, sitting in the brilliant sunshine, which on bright days floods the rooms. "I adore New York, with its beautiful sunshine," she says, with an expressive gesture.

Mme. Landowska, at home, flitting about her rooms, touching lovingly her treasured instruments and souvenirs, seems a different person from the dignified figure, clad in seventeenth century trailing garments, who comes before her audiences to play music of bygone days. Today she wears a simple house gown; her manner is cordial and unaffected, putting her visitors at once at ease. We feel the friendly atmosphere and sip our tea, as we listen to Madame's fluent French, interspersed with German words and phrases, with here and there a touch of English.

"In studying the technic as well as the music for the harpsichord, I had to rely greatly on myself and my own researches," she began. "I had already made a thorough study of the piano and its literature, and we know that technical material for that instrument is endless. But for the clavichord and harpsichord there is nothing, or next to nothing. So I was forced to invent, as it were, my own technical material. If there ever had been works treating of this subject they have long since disappeared. So I had to feel my way and learn through the best means one can have, through experimenting and experience, how to play and interpret the old music.

"Old music has always appealed to me, even as a little child. The other day I played for a whole audience of young students. I looked into their eager faces and said to them:

WANDA LANDOWSKA

" 'I began to play the piano when I was four years old. My first teacher was a kind and indulgent man, who allowed me to browse freely amongst the music which pleased me, which was always music of olden times. I can still remember the delight with which I first heard Bach's Prelude in C major. But, alas, I was soon obliged to change teachers, and the new master proved to be stern and tiresome. I was made to play twenty-five times, each hand separately, the studies of Kalkbrenner and Thalberg, instead of the delightful gavottes and bourrees of Bach, which I loved. Alas, I was very unhappy and homesick for my beloved old-time music. And then I made a vow that I would, one day, when I was grown up, play a program devoted entirely to Bach, Rameau, Haydn and Mozart. I wrote this vow and the program neatly on a sheet of paper, decorated with Christmas pictures, and sealed it in an envelope, on which I wrote "To be opened when I am grown up."

" 'This program and these very pieces are the pieces I am going to play for you today. Do not think that because this music is very learned it must therefore be without feeling. Follow carefully the themes in each hand and you will see how it all sings.

" 'Then listen with all your hearts! Perhaps

this learned but divinely simple music will awaken in you, or in some of you, the same gentle flame that burns in me. Do not be afraid of the grave manner and big wig of Father Bach. Draw near in thought and let us group ourselves about him. You will feel the love, the generous goodness, which fill every phrase of his lovely music. They will unite us by strong and warm ties and enkindle what is good and human within us.'

"And these young people to whom I spoke, listened to the music as I played it, with the greatest interest and attention and seemed to enjoy every note of these compositions of the old masters.

ARE TOUCH AND TECHNIC DIFFERENT ON THE
HARPSICHORD FROM THE PIANO?

"You ask if the touch is different on the harpsichord from what it is on the piano? And in what way? The technic for the harpsichord is much more difficult than for the piano. First of all the touch. Test it for yourself. You see there is great key resistance on the harpsichord. Play a scale now, and you will realize how much more strength of finger is needed and what precision and exactness the player must have.

"The instrument has, as you see, seven pedals,

which help to create the seventy-five varieties of color—*klang-Farben*—of which it is capable. There are two keyboards, of five octaves each, which can be used singly or coupled together. Many people, even those at work in music, do not seem to understand the difference between the clavichord, clavicembalo, harpsichord, clavicin and spinet. The clavichord has but one keyboard, and the old-fashioned square piano is its descendant. Clavicembalo is one of the Italian names for the harpsichord. As I said a moment ago, there are no modern books explaining the manner of playing these old instruments. I had no teacher to help me master their intricacies. I was so anxious to learn that I began a thorough search for old manuscripts, and I found, amid the dust and forgotten tomes of old libraries and museums, much information and knowledge that helped in my quest for technical material and for a comprehension of conditions under which Bach wrote. In this way I caught glimpses of the spirit which animated him and the meaning of his work.

"As to the instrument itself, I conceived that a modern-built harpsichord, which should be reconstructed after the authentic instrument of Bach, ought to be brought out, if we are to make the old music live again. The house of Pleyel,

in Paris, met my wishes, and the result is a very
beautiful instrument, such as you see here. There
are three of these instruments in America now;
this one, which I use in my concerts in New York
and vicinity; one in Philadelphia, and one in
Washington. The instrument in Philadelphia
has black keys where these are white, while the
original black keys are a deep citron yellow. The
harpsichord kept in Washington has keyboards
like this one here; the case, however, is of rich
red wood.

MODERNIZING BACH

"Many authoritative musicians and pianists
have elected to edit Bach's music, with a view to
modernizing it and making it more playable
for today—so they say. Ah, the pity of it! How
dare any one mangle and mutilate these perfect
scores! On this subject I have said in my book,
Music of the Past, 'Change a syllable in a verse
and you make the poem limp.' These editors
efface the image of the most marvelous genius,
on the pretext of bringing it down to date, and
making it more modern.

"Every time a publisher proposes a new edition of a piece on my program, he advises me to
make some changes in it, *so the work may become
our property.* What is even more humiliating is

when an unhappy arranger tries to make us believe that he has made improvements, has renovated a work of Mozart's, sparkling with youth and genius.

"It is really regrettable that even great musicians have been guilty of this offense against genius. Von Bülow said: 'Bach's harpsichord works are the pianist's Old Testament; Beethoven's Sonatas are the New; we should believe in both.' In spite of which he adds measures to the Chromatic Fantasy, and enlarges others; he changes the responses of the Fugue and doubles the basses. Thus, failing to recognize the noble transport and measured passion of the work, he has impregnated it with an alien and theatrical character.

"I do not make these strictures against the transcribers of Bach's organ music for the modern piano, for that is quite another matter. Liszt has greatly contributed to our wealth of piano music by placing these fine works, originally composed for organ, in our hands, and we certainly owe him gratitude for doing so.

EDITIONS OF BACH

"I am often asked what edition of Bach I use. I say at once, none of the modernized publications, in which editors have endeavored to adapt this lovely ancient music to the present-day grand pianos, by making it more sonorous and powerful. No, my Bach must be as pure, as near the spirit in which the master conceived it, as possible. I find the most complete and perfect edition is that of the Bach Gesellschaft, which comes in fifty-six volumes. This I own and it is indeed a treasure."

THE INSTRUMENT

To hear Mme. Landowska describe her instrument is inspiring. She says:

"The harpischord which has been built for me is a wonderful instrument. It has, besides the two keyboards, a great number of registers, imitating the flute, the violin, oboe and even the bagpipe, which vivify the compositions played upon it with the glowing colors of old stained glass. Its deep registers make us feel the dark profoundness of certain preludes and fugues of Bach. The joyous brilliance of its two keyboards, in their struggle with one another, flash and sparkle into flame, and impart to the sonatas of Scarlatti just the right touch of Neapolitan verve. The miracles of jocund grace and of melancholy tenderness which speak to us from the pages of Couperin and Rameau, find again their authentic poetry in that diaphanous sonority."

Thus spoke this remarkable and unique artist, and we listened with rapt attention—over the tea cups. Then, rising, at our request for a portrait, she went to her desk and handed up a photograph of herself, seated before a small upright piano, one of the treasured specimens in her own private collection. It is the instrument which once belonged to Chopin and was used by him during his sojourn at the island of Majorca. As Madame seated herself to write the inscription she had graciously promised, her secretary, a devoted young girl, standing at her elbow, stooped and pressed her lips to the dark head bent over the writing. A pretty touch and one not easily forgotten.

It would be hardly fair to close this brief glimpse of Wanda Landowska without adding a few words about the great work she has done and is now doing for the cause of old-time music. We should not forget that she was first of all a fine pianist, and is now indeed one of the finest we have, a real princess of the keyboard. About her piano playing, one of the critics has said: "To hear her play a Mozart Concerto for the pianoforte is to hear a veritable evocation of the marvelous boy of Salzburg. The perfect continence of her playing, her extraordinary musicianship and finesse, the justness of her accents, her chiseled phrasing, the variety and delicacy of her shading, the soft iridescent coloring of her tone, unite in a magic that transports the listener to a higher and purer region of sound."

As a harpsichordist she is the most distinguished of the present day. And when she is spoken of as an executant of these two instruments, one does not at once consider the enormous amount of study, the deep erudition, the passionate love of the work, which have carried her to such heights.

She has published several books on her chosen subjects. One, *Ancient Music,* which appeared in Paris in 1909, has been translated into English with the title *Music of the Past,* and is published in New York. Mr. Richard Aldrich remarks of it: "Madame Landowska here makes an eloquent defense of the old music. She urges the claims of the elder art, so distinguished by elegance, suppleness, purity of taste, moderation and serene nobility. She dislikes the overwhelming sonorities of these latter days and is not for innovations, for she has sharp words for the way the 'knights of transcription' have taken liberties with harpsichord music."

Among the chapters in *Music of the Past* that

will appeal to present players and teachers are probably those on Style, Tradition, and Interpretation, although every page is interesting and full of suggestion.

X

FREDERIC LAMOND

FIRST REQUISITES FOR A DEPENDABLE PIANO
TECHNIC

At mention of the name Frederic Lamond,
memory carries me back to Berlin in the 80's,
when von Bülow held his memorable Piano Criticism Class, in the studios of Professor Karl
Klindworth. Lamond was a member of that
class. He had come to Berlin with Bülow from
Frankfort. We soon discovered the master considered him a very good pupil indeed; for when,
at times, the playing of other members of the
class did not please him, the young Scot was
called to the piano. He was always able to perform the composition called for in a manner that
the master said was "sehr schön."

Later on, Lamond went to Liszt, and then
began his public career. He concertized all over
Europe and Russia, taught master classes at the
Sondershausen Conservatory, and has found
time, amid much professional activity, to com-

pose a Symphony, chamber music and piano pieces.

Lamond did not come to America until a couple of years ago. After touring the country, he consented to give part of his time to master classes in a great music school.

Possessing a virtuoso pianism, Lamond's interpretations of the greater Beethoven and Liszt are authoritative as well as brilliant. However much the listener may wish for more sentiment at times, he has to admit, in fairness, that he is hearing a master musician of high attainments, who plays with authority and keen understanding.

In discussing pianistic problems with Mr. Lamond, it was found he stands strongly for thorough technical preparedness.

"When it is known I am holding master classes at the Eastman School of Music, I am asked sometimes how I find American pupils as music students. I answer that question by saying they do not seem inclined to come right down to foundational principles and work on their technical equipment, in order to perfect that as much as possible. They do not grasp the importance of technic study outside of repertoire. They think they can learn technic from, let us say, Beethoven's Sonatas, when they should learn it from Czerny. One must do a certain amount of technical study constantly, in order to make any headway with repertoire.

THE LEGATO TOUCH

"One of the first requisites for a dependable technic is to acquire a good *legato;* that is the foundation of everything. We know there are various kinds of legato. There is the perfectly connected touch, the overlapping touch, and the slightly detached or non-legato touch. All these should be understood and under control. Perhaps the best material to use for developing discriminating touch—when one is far enough developed—is the Well-Tempered Clavichord, of Bach. Think of the Second Prelude, for instance; it develops precision and clean finger action. Several varieties of legato can be used in it. The Fugue teaches variety of touch, tone and phrasing. Number 3 I might call a lady's Prelude and Fugue; it is indeed charming.

"It is a curious fact that only a few of these Preludes and Fugues seem to be familiar, even to serious students. When do we ever hear the one in G, or the last pair in Book I? And Book II is less known than Book I. I use both books equally. A knowledge of this great music is in itself a liberal education to any student. I do not mean simply being able to play a few of them from the notes. I mean to be familiar with them all so thoroughly as to master their structure and content, and, of course, to know them from memory.

TECHNICAL MATERIAL

"Other technical material should include the Henselt Études. They are excellent for wide reaches and stretches, and they are far too little known. Henselt has a genius for devising all sorts of finger reaches as technical exercises, and his Études are very helpful in all such ways.

"The advanced student must finally develop his own technic, according to the structure of his hand and, I might add, according to his own mentality. We really do not find any two artists playing the piano in exactly the same way. Leschetizky made a specialty of technical training, yet each of his pianists plays differently from the others. Take three names at random—Slivinsky, Gabrilowitsch and Schnabel. They each have an individual technic, which they have evolved to fit their own requirements.

"In order to cultivate a Chopin or Liszt technic, I have learned that the thumb plays a very vital rôle. I might say that the thumb, in more ways than one, is the pivotal point in playing.

Hardly any student comprehends that the thumb should be free to move from its knuckle joint, which is to be found at its base. Knowing this, the attention can then be directed to cultivating lateral movements of thumb, which can move *out* and *under* the hand, while the hand can move *over* and *back* from the thumb. In this way the thumb acts as a pivot to throw the hand over and back, as in scales and arpeggios, or in skips.

THE AMATEUR

"The musical amateur 'loves music,' and loves to talk about music. She is easily swayed, at a concert, by signs of the sentimental in a performer, and applauds, even though she may at the same time be listening to constant sins against good taste and correctness. How does she know when there is too much *rubato,* when a phrase is distorted, when notes are made longer or shorter than they are written? Even many of the critics do not know these things, so why expect her to be wiser than they?

"The musical amateur studies music—in her way—and her desire for sentimental tone is seen in the way she delivers a melody, for she presses the key with unction, and then makes a vibrating movement of hand after the key is depressed— much as a violinist or 'cellist makes the quivering movement on the string. She imagines this shaking of the hand is going to make the tone more expressive and soulful. When she plays octaves her hands are flat, wrists high and all fingers outstretched. She cannot seem to grasp the idea that the hand should be held in a somewhat arched position, with fingers slightly curved, to avoid hitting other keys, or the name-board.

"I merely mention these as a few of the little things we teachers have to struggle with in the pupils who come to us.

EARLY YEARS

"I have had a rather unique experience in my musical up-bringing. In the beginning I was trained as a violinist. Of course I learned a little piano along with my violin study, but it was intended I should stick to the violin. Yes, like Harold Bauer in this regard, though I am sure he was a much better violinist than I ever was. All the same, I played rather respectably. I learned to play the organ, too, in my early years. When I was about fourteen, I was sent to the Raff Conservatory at Frankfort, where I studied violin under Heerman, piano with Schwarz, and composition with Urspruch. Later, when von Bülow came to Frankfort, I decided to give up violin and devote myself wholly to the piano. I wanted to have lessons with Bülow, but I knew he was a very difficult mentality to deal with. However, I made the attempt, and finally entered his class. He said little when I played, as it was not his way, and I feared from this that he was entirely indifferent. But I learned a little later that he was kindly disposed toward me. Of course I was just a young boy in those days, but knowing something of the violin and even a little about the oboe, I was always spending my spare time about the orchestra, listening to the rehearsals, and to whatever else was going on. In this way the master's attention was often directed to me. It was a wonderful education to see and hear Bülow conduct. What precision, what endless care for every little point! His aim was perfection from the smallest detail up.

"I worked very hard with my piano repertoire, for I had much to do to catch up. When I was sixteen or seventeen, my master went to Berlin for the month of May, to conduct a master class at his friend Karl Klindworth's Conservatory. He asked me to accompany him.

"The Klindworths had a fine house in one of the best parts of the city, and the Professor had a large following, with quite a number of American students among them. The class assembled every morning, the session lasting from eight-thirty till twelve-thirty or one o'clock. Only the works of Raff, Mendelssohn, Brahms and Liszt were to be played; no Beethoven, Chopin or Schumann, for, as Bülow said, he had to hear the music of those composers constantly in Frankfort, and he wanted a change of thought when he came to Berlin. He gave much attention to the compositions of Raff, and we had to do the Suites, of which there are two or three good ones. I am afraid, in spite of all, that the music of Raff will not be resuscitated in the future, though it has so many excellent qualities.

THE BULOW CLASS

"Brahms may be said to have been the favorite composer of the session. We had the Haendel Variations, the Ballades, Rhapsodies, Capriccios and Intermezzi. I was called upon to play the Variations and Fugue, so it will be seen I must have worked pretty hard to have been able to manage this difficult composition.

"Of Liszt we did the Ballades and some of the big Études. That one which he calls *Feu Follets* is a tricky little thing—though really not little either, and splendid work for fourth and fifth fingers. One can almost acquire a special technic for those two fingers out of it.

"After the May class was over, at the very end of the month, I returned to Frankfort and resumed my studies with Bülow, who now showed me many kindnesses. Later in the season I went to the little town of Meiningen, where Bülow conducted the famous Meiningen Orchestra. If you have ever seen and heard him as conductor, you know what a master he was. He not only directed from memory, but expected his men to know their parts by heart. He also made the men stand the entire time through a concert, remarking that, as he was obliged to be on his feet all the time the band should also be able to do likewise.

"I managed to slip in and hear many rehearsals and so learned a great deal about the orchestra. I was present when Brahms' new Symphony was put in rehearsal. It seems that Brahms had lately finished this Symphony—the Fourth. On its completion, he had wrapped it up and sent it to Bülow by ordinary post. One morning Bülow came to rehearsal in a terrific state of excitement. At first no one seemed to know what was the matter. At last it began to be comprehended that the MS. of the Brahms Symphony had gone astray, perhaps had been lost. All was consternation. Brahms himself was appealed to. No, he had no duplicate copy, and if the work were really lost, he would have to rewrite it from memory.

"But after a time of anxious suspense the MS. turned up and was put in rehearsal. It was found to be very difficult and much time was needed to prepare it. I well remember the first performance, when the work was presented to a very musical audience. As soon as all was over and the audience had dispersed, Brahms sent word he wished the Symphony repeated at once. The members of the orchestra were hurriedly recalled and took their places in the darkened concert hall. Brahms himself conducted. It was an occasion never to be forgotten. The figure of the composer, with his long hair and flowing beard, his right arm holding the baton raised aloft, was silhouetted against the light of the platform. And thus the great work was heard twice in succession that same day.

"Ah, those were happy days, not to come again. I studied with Liszt also in that youthful time, and one day I will tell you more about it."

XI

ERNO VON DOHNANYI

TECHNICAL MATERIAL DISCUSSED

A SERIOUS, thoughtful, earnest musician is Erno Von Dohnanyi, Hungarian composer-pianist. He seems to be equally at home in the field of composition and conductorship as when giving a recital on the concert stage. Acknowledged one of the big pianists of the day, he is also a composer who has contributed various graceful as well as grateful pieces to the pianists' repertoire, and last, but not least, he is a conductor of originality and virility.

America has had several visits from this artist. The first came in the season of 1898-9, when he was only twenty-one. He returned two years later for another tour. Then came a long break, of about twenty years, during which Dohnanyi continued his European tours, and then was appointed Professor of Piano Playing in the Royal Hochschule, in Berlin, a post he held for eleven years. He now resides in Budapest. Fully occupied with professional duties, composition, and

104

ERNO VON DOHNANYI

prevented by the World War from leaving home,
he was unable to return to America until a couple
of years ago. We then found him a matured
pianist and composer.

AS A TEACHER

As a teacher, Dohnanyi has a large following,
and has directed the studies and developed the
talents of various well-known pianists. "Dohnanyi is such a wonderful master, and above all
such a thorough musician. I know of no greater
teacher, if the pupil is well prepared and able
to profit by such guidance." This is the testi-
mony of Mischa Levitzki, who was a student of
the Hungarian master, in Berlin, for a considerable time. There are other students in this
country, and many more who both admire and
play his compositions. The four Rhapsodies are
becoming familiar in our concert rooms, while
the *Winterreigen,* a charming set of piano pieces,
was played by Rudolph Reuter a couple of seasons ago in New York. We know that Brahms
praised the compositions of Dohnanyi. Besides
the pieces already mentioned, there is a piano
Concerto, which is excellently well conceived for
the instrument, and other works of an ideal character.

In a conversation with Dohnanyi, some questions were asked in regard to handling various grades of pupils.

"I firmly believe in individuality in piano teaching. Each pupil is a different mentality and forms a separate study. My own case would not be that of any one else. A piano method which works well for one pupil might not be the best for another. It is true a desired result may be attained through different means, and these means should be adapted to the needs of each pupil.

"Of course, in the early stages, one must be well-grounded in finger exercises, scales, arpeggios and octaves. There is nothing that will quite take the place of scales, to gain fluency and command of the keyboard. As the student advances, he should be given a liberal amount of Bach. A selection of Czerny is also indispensable. Then comes Clementi; we cannot do without him either, if we are to help the pupil to build a thoroughly furnished background.

"To this end an adequate familiarity with the classics is necessary. Mozart, Haydn, even Hummel, are not to be neglected. Mozart has left numerous Sonatas, Concertos and several Fantaisies; some of these are very beautiful, especially the Fantaisies, and are of the greatest value in forming the student's taste. The Sonatas of

Haydn, also, are perhaps even richer in technical
and musical material.

"The keeping up of my own technic and repertoire is perhaps a case of what I do not do. At
present I spend little time on abstract routine
technical exercises, as so many pianists think
they must do, for that seems to me a waste of
time, which is so precious to the musician. Of
course, as you know, every pianist has some little mechanical forms, which he uses to oil up his
machinery, so to speak; but that is an individual
matter. I can truly say I have never practised
technic exhaustively. I began to play the piano
at the age of six, and even in those early days
read much at sight and played with other instruments. Thus I gradually evolved a technic
of my own at the instrument.

"It goes without saying that one can waste
much time over so-called technical material, and
not really get anywhere, or make a definite advance. It can be merely useless repetition. Of
the books on pure technic, like Hanon and
Pischna, I prefer the latter. It has been said a
player ought to be able to go through Hanon in
one hour—what a grind!

"Everything depends on *how* one practises.
One student may spend five hours at the piano
and will not accomplish as much or progress as

fast as one who spends one hour at work, but concentrates his whole mind on the task before him. The first is a mechanical machine, the second uses his mental powers.

"One of the best ways to keep up one's technic as well as one's repertoire is, I have found, to select the difficult portions of compositions, and make technical studies out of them. The literature of the piano provides such rich material of all kinds that the student or artist need never be at a loss.

AS TO ÉTUDES

"I should like to offer a protest against using too many études, for much valuable time may be thus wasted. Students often think the greater number of études they go through, the better players they will be; whereas they had much better put some of that time on mastering repertoire. What masses of études have been written! Their name is legion. Von Bülow edited a book of fifty Cramer Studies, selecting those he considered the best. But while the player is learning these, he could put in the time to more advantage on pieces of value, which would add just so much to his repertoire.

"Of course some of the études are very nice, but we have grown away, in these modern days,

from the older ways of study. We do not seem
to need so many studies, nor do we use them in
the way a past generation did. If, however, you
speak of the Études of Chopin, that is quite another matter. Chopin Études belong to the
repertoire of every pianist; indeed they are not
études at all but beautiful works of art, which
every one must love. In them one finds every
form of technical problem, which is necessary for
the building up of a virtuoso pianism. Why
should one seek afar, when such wonderful material is ready to the hand? Of course, they are
not for the immature student. For all who attempt to master them must be prepared through
the practise of scales, chords, octaves, and so on."

Although Dohnanyi does not concern himself
with the technical preparation of the students
and players who come to him—artist-teachers
are not expected to do this—he is very painstak-
ing and careful in his teaching. He regards the
subject of artistic interpretation as of the very
highest importance. It is the soul of the music
which interests and absorbs him completely, not
the body of mere mechanical notes and signs.
The meaning and spirit of the music is what he
seeks to reveal to the student. Again to quote
from Mischa Levitski, his admiring pupil:

"When I went to Dohnanyi, he first gave me

the smaller things, such as the Kinderscenen of Schumann and the earliest Sonatas of Beethoven. He believes the player should have much more technic than the music one is studying requires, so he usually gives pieces that do not tax too severely the technical ability of the player, in order that he may more fully grasp and master the meaning of the piece. At the lesson he allows the student to play through the work in hand without interruption, listening carefully, and often jotting inaccuracies and corrections on a slip of paper, though he generally tries to remember them. When the composition is finished—not before—he makes the necessary corrections. Finally he himself plays the piece entirely through. As he is such a master of interpretation, this of itself is a great inspiration to the pupil."

Dohnanyi is very particular about clearness of touch, requiring slow and careful practise, with fingers well raised. The beginning and finish of a phrase, its shading and climaxes are all carefully considered.

Asked if he were familiar with American music, especially the compositions of Edward MacDowell, he admitted he had seen very little of it, and did not know the Sonatas at all. He had, however, become initiated into the intricacies

of American jazz, which, he said, is for the head
and not for the heart. He considers it intellectual and not emotional.

The human side of an artist is the side the
general public does not guess; in the case of this
artist it is a very lovable side. I remember meeting him one evening in the side corridor of Carnegie Hall, at the close of a recital by Levitzki.
A long program had been given, with many encores added. The master had remained to hear
them all. He wanted to go to the artist's room,
greet his popular pupil and then leave. There
was an eager look on his tired face. But no, another encore was demanded, and granted; so he
turned into the hall again, to wait patiently for
the last.

On another occasion, hearing that the music
committee of the MacDowell Club had arranged
an entire Bach program, he asked if he might
contribute something to it. We joyfully consented, of course. He came and played the
Chromatic Fantaisie and Fugue, adding another
Bach number as an encore. It was a graceful
thing to do, and everybody appreciated his kindness.

He has a keen sense of humor, too, in spite of
his grave demeanor. Looking from the windows
of the office building in which are the rooms of

his managers, he spied the Y. M. C. A. Building, on the side wall of which are painted various signs, two of which read: "Men's Bible Class"— "Swimming Pool."

"Where but in America would one see those terms in conjunction?" he remarked, with his faint smile.

ALEXANDER SILOTI

GLIMPSES OF RUBINSTEIN AND LISZT

ALEXANDER SILOTI, the eminent Russian pianist and musician, a favorite pupil and friend of Liszt, a relative of Rachmaninoff, whose name —known everywhere—stands for what is dignified, noble and best in musical art, is living among us, walking our streets, visiting our concert halls, and learning—we hope—to feel at home in the new land. He does not, however, assimilate the language of the country of his adoption, for he insists he cannot learn English. But he converses readily in German, and is full of reminiscence of the many wonderful musical experiences of an eventful life, a few of which he has imparted to me at different times and occasions.

"Some of the happiest, although some of the most strenuous, days of my student life were spent with the master, Franz Liszt, in Weimar. I was but a lad of nineteen, and not long before had finished my course of study at the Conservatory of Moscow. At the completion of this course I was to have some lessons with Anton Rubinstein, who offered to give me occasional lessons whenever he came to Moscow to conduct the symphony concerts.

"Those lessons were very strenuous, to say the least. I heard I was to prepare four great works for my first lesson. They were: Schumann's *Kreisleriana,* Beethoven's Emperor Concerto and Sonata Op. 101, and, to cap the climax, Chopin's Sonata in B minor. I knew none of these works and had but about six weeks to prepare them. At the end of that time, by practising seven or eight hours a day, I really learned the notes at least, if not much of the meaning.

"The events of the first lesson are stamped on my memory. The master was not alone, but a number of society ladies were present. 'Play,' said Rubinstein. I chose the *Kreisleriana,* and began, expecting him to stop me at any moment. He never said one word, but allowed me to continue through the whole piece, of eight parts. When I finished at last, there was absolute silence, which made me feel as though I had lost everything.

"At last he rose and came to the piano. 'Kreisler was a wonderful man who possessed great poetic feeling, combined with a tremendous

ALEXANDER SILOTI

amount of "temperament." What you have to do is to play these pieces so that every one will realize this fact.' Then, seating himself at the instrument, he played the *Kreisleriana* as one inspired. The young student was entirely forgotten: he was too insignificant to take any notice of. I felt as though I should give up the study of music for all time. I could not help contrasting this treatment with the manner of Nicholas Rubinstein, who had also been my teacher. His method was to play to his pupils in such a way that they were able to realize the ideal he set before them. He took into consideration the amount of talent each student possessed, and inspired him with the hope that he would be able, one day, to play as well as his teacher.

"There were other lessons of the same sort with Anton Rubinstein, which, as I look back on them, seem like nightmares. If the desire to learn was not killed in me it was due to my happy disposition.

"At last it was made possible for me to go abroad for further study, which I hoped might be with the great master Liszt. Even Anton Rubinstein felt that the greatest thing for me would be to be accepted as a pupil by Liszt.

"A couple of friends traveled with me, and we arrived in Leipsic in time for the Music Festival, in which Liszt himself was taking part. I met him and he asked me to come to Weimar and study with him. As soon as the Festival was over, my friends went with me to Weimar, and engaged a room for me there. By this time I was horribly homesick, for I knew not a word of German. After my first lesson with the master, however, this feeling left me and I threw myself into my studies with the greatest ardor. For three years thereafter I had the infinite privilege of coming into close contact, both as pupil and friend, with this wonderful man, who showed me many marks of his kindly interest and affectionate regard.

CHARACTERISTICS OF LISZT'S PLAYING

"I am asked sometimes what were the distinguishing characteristics of Liszt's playing, and why it was so remarkable. The question is somewhat difficult to answer. His piano tone was not so big; some of the rest of us had as much; but it excelled in a marvelous searching quality, the poignancy of which I have never heard from any one else. In fact, it could not be said that he merely played the piano, but rather that he played *music*. For the terms are widely different. He would sit at the very same piano which we students would thump with our playing, a very mediocre, unreliable thing; yet he would produce music from it such as we, none of us, had dreamed of. Apropos of Anton Rubinstein, Liszt once told me a story of a banquet given to Rubinstein in Vienna, at the close of his series of historical concerts there, Liszt himself being present. One of the committee gave 'Rubinstein' as the first toast. Rubinstein became very restless during the speech, and as soon as it was finished he sprang to his feet, exclaiming, 'How can you drink to my health, or honor me as a pianist, when Liszt is sitting among us. Compared to him we are all corporals and he is the one and only Field-Marshal!'

"Whoever heard Anton Rubinstein has heard a fine artist—a great artist. I studied with him and know whereof I speak. Compared with the rest of us, he towered far higher. We were pigmies and he the stalwart man. But when one speaks of Liszt, then Rubinstein sinks into insignificance. He is then the pigmy and Liszt the giant. As much difference between them as between black and white. While Rubinstein had a fine tone quality, which he diligently cultivated, Liszt's tone was memorable, unforgettable. I shall never forget how he intoned the theme of the first movement of Beethoven's *Moonlight Sonata*. The memory of those tones will remain with me for life; I can hear them now and always try to reproduce them when I play the work.

LISZT'S MUSIC

"It is the fashion to play Liszt's music, and many treat it very superficially, as though it were merely meant for the salon. But there is usually a deeper meaning than appears on the surface. The master generally had some special thought or experience, which influenced or compelled him to compose as he did. The interpreter of his music must bring to it a many-sided experience of life in order to fathom its depths.

"Take, for instance, that short composition of his, *Il Penseroso*. To many pianists it means little or nothing; just a 'harmony of sweet sounds.' When he wrote it, Liszt had in mind that masterpiece of Michael Angelo, the statue of Lorenzo di Medici, in the Church of San Lorenzo in Florence. It will be remembered that he sits, a heroic figure, plunged in deep reflection, above two recumbent figures at his feet. The work is termed 'Meditation,' and is one of the great marbles of the world of art. So with Liszt's *Sposolizio,* an embodiment, in tones, of Raphael's masterpiece of the Madonna. One has only to turn to these pieces, to which Liszt has given titles, to realize the poetical signifi-

cance of the poetical nature of the compositions.
I carry photographs of these masterpieces with
me as reminders of the master's intentions.

"In my long life I have met many interesting
and remarkable personalities, but never have I
seen any one as impressive as Liszt. One felt
the instant one came in touch with him that there
was something majestic, god-like in him; one
felt that here was an all-embracing spirit. He
impressed people that way and he played music
in that spirit—the spirit of a conqueror.

LISZT THE TEACHER

"Liszt taught in quite a different way from
any one else. He generally sat beside, or stood
opposite to, the student who was playing, and
indicated by the expression of his face the nu-
ances he wanted brought out in the music. For
the first few months I had lessons with the others
in class; afterwards I had lessons alone. Of
course I knew each work I brought to him, so that
I was able to watch his face for signs of interpretation.

"No other master could indicate musical
phrasing as he could, merely by the expression
of his face. If the student understood these fine
shades, so much the better—for him. Liszt felt
he could explain nothing to pupils who did not

understand him from the first. Each student brought whatever composition he wished, as Liszt never told us what to work on.

"There were two pieces we were not allowed to bring, however; the *Moonlight Sonata,* of Beethoven and Liszt's Second Rhapsodie. Another one he did not care for was Chopin's Scherzo in B flat minor, which he jestingly called the 'Governess Scherzo.' Everything else of Chopin's, especially the Preludes, he delighted to hear. He insisted on a poetical interpretation, and it irritated him when groups of small notes were played too quickly.

THE MUSIC OF BACH

"How Liszt loved the music of Bach, and taught us all to love it with him! I am still a student of this great music, for I do not yet know all of it, by any means. I am only beginning to realize and feel its deep, inner meaning. I was over forty years old before I arrived at an understanding of the true greatness of the master, and learned to play his music more in the way it should be played. Young pianists nowadays are fond of placing some of these big works on their programs. Well and good; if they play the notes with clearness and precision, and give a general idea of the form of the com-

positions. When I see these programs I say—
if the player is young—no, he has not *lived,* he
has not the life experience to play such music.
When one is twenty one cannot fathom the mys-
teries of Bach. Neither at thirty. At forty, one
begins to understand; at forty-five—yes, at forty-
five, one should have arrived at years of experience—of life. But, lest these words should
discourage young students and players who like
to play Bach's music, I hasten to say that I encourage them to study much and deeply into the
works of this great master, for this study will
bear rich fruit one day, when experience has prepared the soil and fertilized it.

AMERICA SHOULD DEVELOP GREAT MUSIC

"I feel, when I come to America, this great
young country, that its people are strong, full
of fire and vitality; for this reason they should
also develop great music. In the Old World all
depends on tradition; the people are bound and
held back by it. They speak, act and feel as
their parents, their grandparents, their great-
grandparents felt and acted. They are held back
by barriers and obstacles of custom. Young
America meets the obstacle fairly, gives it a
blow, pushes it aside and rushes on. Because
their ancestors, in the old country, heated their

houses very inadequately and froze in cold weather, their descendants do the same. America is more progressive and aggressive; the present generation will not follow in the steps of its forbears, but believes in progress. I love this freedom to progress, to constantly climb higher, and I feel this spirit will animate the art-life of the nation.

MANNER OF PRACTISE

"Yes, I practise slowly. It is true that fast practise is the bane of many a young student. Slow practise, with medium power, not full power. I do not now practise scales and finger exercises, but rather passages from pieces—difficult portions and places from the whole literature of the piano, or, perhaps I should say, from my own repertoire. Take the C sharp major Prelude, from Bach's *Well-tempered Clavichord;* that makes a fine finger study. Then parts of the Chopin Études, octaves from Tschaikowsky, or anything that exercises the various muscles, or bits that need constant repetition. One must always be at work—always practising; an artist can never get away from that.

"As it may have been noticed from my recital programs, I have edited and revised many compositions, adapting them in various ways to

the needs of the modern pianist. I have a large
hand, with a wide span, and do not need to re-
sort to the necessities of small hands in playing.
For instance, take the little Gigue in B flat, by
Bach. It will be remembered that this short
piece requires constant crossing of left hand over
the right, in order to bring out the melody. This
effort is really not necessary, if one has a hand
capable of reaching the intervals. I have altered
the manner of performing the notes between the
two hands, so there is seldom any crossing of
hands necessary. In this way the piece is quite
simple, and there is no change in the notes themselves. In fact the theme sings itself more con-
nectedly through this manner of playing. Many
compositions gain in ease of delivery by forethought in making them more pianistic and help-
ing them to lie better under the hands.

THOROUGH STUDY OF MUSIC

"I have very definite ideas as to how music
should be taught. Let me tell you how we do
it in Russia, in the great Conservatories there.

"Everything goes by system. There are two
classes of students, the Lower and the Upper;
there are also two classes of instructors. Those
for the earlier grades must understand the
foundation very thoroughly, and must carry the

student from the first beginnings up to a certain point, when he is ready to enter the higher classes. The Lower Class instructor may or may not be a player; he can cover the elementary work without ever having come before the public as a pianist. His office is that of a teacher.

"The Upper Class master is called a Professor. He must be a concert artist, either actively before the public, or one who has done concert work at one time of his career. He builds up the student on the foundation laid by the assistant teacher, and aims to turn the student out an artistic player and good musician. The Professor trains him in advanced repertoire, forms his taste, and should be able to act as an interpretive model worthy of imitation.

"There is also system in the study of repertoire. Take the Lower Class, for instance. It has several divisions. For each of these a certain number of compositions must be studied, such as are suitable for that degree of advancement. Small programs, for each division, can be made from these earlier lists. As the student advances, his repertoire grows with his progress. He must study for two years before he attempts anything of Chopin. As for Beethoven—with the exception of the little Sonatines and small pieces—a full-fledged Sonata is not to be thought of for a number of years. Thus the student is carefully grounded, grows slowly but surely, and advances gradually into the stature of a well-rounded musician.

"Perhaps you may think this sounds too slow and pedantic for the rapidly moving American. It may be somewhat slow, but it is thorough; it forms sound musicianship and produces capable artists. Russia is not alone in desiring thoroughness, for these methods are followed in other European music schools. The result of this artistic completeness is that Americans, in many cases, have felt it necessary to come to Europe to study. Why do they do so? Because they realize that there is more thorough and artistic training to be had abroad than at home. But there is really no need for this condition to exist. If Americans felt they could get equally sound, thorough and artistic culture at home, there would be no reason for them to seek it elsewhere.

THE GENERAL MUSIC SCHOOL

"It seems to me we have to look deeper than the curriculum of the foreign music school— deeper even than its artistic ideals, to find the cause of its artistic standing and success. The crux of the matter really is that the big European music schools are not run for pecuniary profit; they do not exist to make money. There is always a deficit at the end of the year. If the school is subsidized, the Government attends to the deficit; if not, wealthy individuals or a committee in charge of school affairs looks after it. It is art first with us in Russia, *not* to see how much money can be made out of teachers' labor, or out of students' fees.

"The case is different in America, is it not? There may be a few endowed music schools with you. But the general run of conservatories follow the plan of building upon a financial foundation—in other words, of *making it pay*.

"I have conferred with some of the heads of flourishing schools in this country, and they all tell me the same thing. They say: 'Our school is on a firm financial basis; it brings in large sums each year; we never have a deficit.' And I say to them: 'It is not possible to run a school with the highest ideals, which will do justice to its professors, its teachers and students, and yet make money. The money you make comes out of the teacher, who slaves day in and day out, in order that the institution may take half the fee he earns from the student, and thus make money for it.' I say to them frankly: 'I cannot teach in any institution under such conditions. Not that I wish to make large sums for myself; I am satisfied to earn enough for daily needs.'

"It is the same with orchestras everywhere. They cannot be run for profit; there must always be sound financial backing. An illustration from my own experience might be apropos. I arranged a performance of a large work of Ducasse for chorus and orchestra. In order to secure musicians, hall, advertising and rehearsals, the expenses were 11,000 rubles. Tickets brought 5,500 rubles, leaving half the expenses to come out of my own pocket.

"Therefore, I repeat, it is impossible to give concerts of the highest class, or run an ideal music school, at a profit. Have the latter endowed; found it on the highest ideals, and you would have supreme institutions right in your midst.

"I am very glad to say a few words on this question; for I feel it is a vital one in the cause of music in this country."

XIII

ELIE ROBERT SCHMITZ

THE INTERPRETATION OF MODERN FRENCH
MUSIC

WHAT wonderful artificers are the French in
the line of virtuoso instrumentalists at the piano!
E. Robert Schmitz, a representative of the brilliant school of French pianism, has made his
home in America for several years, and through
frequent recitals and lectures has taught us much
about the music of his country.

A couple of weeks after his arrival in America,
he demonstrated, in a recital at the MacDowell
Club, that he possessed a prodigious technic,
which included power, delicacy, velocity and brilliancy. More than these, there is much variety
of tone and real native *esprit*.

I had the opportunity of coming into touch
with the French artist very shortly after he came
here, and we had an interesting conference over
the subjects in which he was most deeply concerned.

Mr. Schmitz has the record of serving his

ELIE ROBERT SCHMITZ

country from the very beginning of the war. For thirty-eight months he was on the firing-line, including the Somme, Verdun and Chemin des Dames. What could he not tell of life in the trenches! Several times wounded, the last of his misfortunes was to be gassed. Then came six months in a hospital, to recuperate and get back health and strength. Finally the Government released him from active service and has permitted him, instead, to come to America "to make propaganda for French music," as he smilingly puts it. "I am authorized to tell you and to show you as much as I can of what French composers have accomplished and are now doing.

"To begin at the beginning," he continued, "I was born in Alsace. My mother was an Italian, with a beautiful voice, my father was French. So I unite the characteristics of the two nations.

"I began music study early, with two instruments, piano and violin. Both these I kept up for several years, until I entered the Paris Conservatoire. Here I studied piano with Diémer. I worked very hard, both for my professors and on the outside as well, for I wanted to turn my musical knowledge to account. For one thing, I played accompaniments for many singers, and in this way attracted the notice of Debussy. From that moment I did much work with him, for he took a real interest in me. I went over all his piano pieces with him, playing them according to his ideas. He would show me the sketches and talk over his new compositions with me when they were finished, or even before they were completed. I can truthfully say, I know Debussy's music from A to Z; more than this, I know every note from memory. This means not only the music for the piano, but for the voice, for other instruments and the opera *Pelléas et Mélisande* as well. And what I have done for Debussy's music, in committing and making it my own, I have done also for other French composers—Fauré, César Franck, Louis Aubert, d'Indy and others.

"I continued to do more and more outside work, until I left the Conservatoire, to make my own career. I then toured England, Belgium, Germany and Italy. In Paris I organized a choral society and later, in 1912, founded a new concert orchestra numbering ninety, forty-five of whom were prize-winners at the Conservatoire, so they were all young men. From this body of orchestral players I made several smaller groups, among them a string quartet; while from the chorus I chose a vocal quartet. The concerts we gave created something of a sensation through their programs, which were devoted mainly to

French music. Here are a few of these programs I have brought with me, one in which I collaborated with Debussy, d'Indy and Aubert, both as conductor and soloist. Here are also piano programs which feature the music of my country mingled with some Belgian, Russian and Scandinavian. For in France I endeavored to make known some of the works of other European countries, just as here in America I will confine myself mostly to French music."

Many questions crowded the mind of the listener during this interesting recital, a few of which were asked:

"How did I keep up my technic? As I have already said, I did nothing with my piano playing for nearly four years. Once or twice we found a piano which the Germans had abandoned somewhere, and we tried to make a little music on it, but that was all the chance we ever had. Once, in the hospital, I gave a short recital. When I was at last released and could get to work, I got my technic back in three days. I really do not have to practise technic as some others do; it may be because I have solved many of its problems. Formerly I used to be stiff and tense, until I learned to understand the principles of weight and relaxation. Very quick action with high curved fingers causes weariness and stiffness, whereas the fall of the finger from the knuckle-joint is much less fatiguing. There are two active centers of movement in piano playing—the wrist-joint and the knuckle-joint. I have learned to keep my mechanism in good working condition by means of movements of these joints. It is not necessary for me to practise these movements at the piano, for I can do them better away from the instrument. As we know, the cords and ligaments which control the hands and fingers pass through the wrist. I make many movements of hand at the wrist, which keep this joint in working condition, more so than if I merely exercised my fingers at the piano. I also move all fingers once up and down at the knuckle-joint, which action develops them with less exertion than finger action used at the piano with exercises would require. Then I have various gymnastic stretching, bending and twisting stunts for the fingers themselves. So that, with all these, I can keep myself in condition, even if deprived of the use of an instrument. I must add, however, that these exercises are particularly adapted to my own hand and fingers. They were born of necessity and might not prove beneficial to others.

"Yes, I have made thorough studies in theory and composition, and have various compositions in my portfolio. But they are not ready to see the light. They are quietly waiting and maturing. I prefer for the present to come before the American people as a pianist, and possibly later as a conductor, if opportunity should offer. I had just completed a set of lecture recitals in Chicago before coming to New York. These were, of course, on modern French music. At the first lecture there were only twenty-five or thirty people present; at the second about seventy; at the third over a hundred. And so the interest grew. At each lecture I played a program, explaining the meaning of the music. I expect to do the same here and in other cities."

Mr. Schmitz has ably fulfilled his intentions. He has, indeed, played recitals and given lectures in many cities and has held classes in various parts of the country. He has won for himself and his art a distinctive place in the musical activities of America. As a teacher, too, he has a large following. His is distinctively the school of modern French pianism, graceful yet vigorous in style, full of variety of light and shade, abounding in vivid accents and, at times, in amazing power and velocity.

It is difficult to define just what is meant by the school of French pianism. In the playing of Guiomar Novaes we discover certain movements of finger and arm, certain conditions of muscles, which create special tone qualities. As she was trained in Paris, her style is one phase of the French school. Cortot shows another side to French pianism, a side we have learned to deeply admire. His style is also French.

Robert Schmitz presents yet another view of French pianistic art. He goes further than the others in lightness of finger and absolute looseness of wrist and arm. He seeks to show the student how to acquire both delicacy and great power, through the necessary conditions and movements which he claims will produce these effects. He is a pianist of special and unique charm, and a teacher of recognized sincerity and ability.

Mr. Schmitz came to my studio on a subsequent occasion for further conference on pianistic themes.

"Many players come to me for advice and instruction, and I always find something lacking in them: there are always holes in their equipment which need to be filled up or bridged over. It often happens that there are certain muscles and ligaments in the hand and arm which have never been used, but which are needed in playing the piano. My studies into the causes of musical effects and variety of sounds, show me that the principle of balance is little understood. If I throw back my hand at right angles with the wrist, the muscles on the upper side of the arm are pulling the hand back, while the under muscles are being stretched. When the hand descends on the keys, the reverse action happens to the two sets of muscles. For powerful, brilliant octaves, we make use of the principle of balance, and acquire power through great swiftness of stroke, combined with drawing the end fingers together. This quick action causes the hand to rebound from the keys, giving brilliancy with little effort. An exaggerated form of this principle, or exercise, causes the hand to rebound with fingers very much curved." Mr. Schmitz claims this principle, if practised slowly in octaves, will give a development that nothing else can, and will color rapid octave passages.

Another principle, that of permitting the pedal to create legato effects instead of connecting with the fingers, was thoroughly discussed. The pianist used many illustrations at the piano to prove that the former idea created atmosphere and often brilliancy, which are lacking in the older method.

"If you want fingers to connect tones, in slow tempo, you touch the keys with slow pressure. There is no brilliancy in such a touch as that;

you may not wish for it. If you do, you must make quicker movements—much quicker. If you desire brilliancy with atmosphere, then take your fingers off the keys and allow the strings to vibrate with the pedal.

"Sometimes you need a powerful, virile note. Make it with a swift descent of arm upon the key, which arrests its descent only enough to sound the tone, while the arm continues its swift fall below the keyboard. The tone sounded is at the half-way point, so to speak, of the movement."

Mr. Schmitz also demonstrated different qualities of tone in heavy chords. One effect is made by playing *away* from the body, using the weight of the body to give sonority to the impact. Another effect is produced by reversing the movement and drawing the hands and arms *toward* the body. Still another quality of tone is achieved by descending perpendicularly upon the keys. Some of these touches yield exceedingly brilliant and even harsh effects; but these are sometimes necessary for the sake of variety and to give the sense of extreme vehemence.

The "slapping touch" was discussed. Mr. Schmitz believes this touch—a mere impulse of the natural weight of a flat finger—represents the least effort that can be made. At first—to acquire it—make a slight slap on the key, without tone. When this can be done very lightly and without effort, proceed to make a tone with the slap, which will cause the finger to rebound. Thus it begins to seem that the key release forces the finger up—almost as though the key itself were doing the work, so effortless is the movement of finger. Mr. Schmitz * believes in putting no more effort than necessary into piano technic —in fact, to do everything with the greatest ease. In powerful passages one would imagine, in watching him, that great force was being used. But he maintains that everything has become automatic, therefore done with little or no effort.

"We need every variety of tone color," he says, "produced by every form of touch, in order to play the piano convincingly. The more resources we have, the greater command we achieve over the music and over ourselves."

* The piano classes held by Mr. Schmitz in different parts of the country have been interesting to students and teachers. For further information in regard to these and the compositions interpreted see the author's "What to Play—What to Teach," pages 271-281 (Presser).

XIV

NICHOLAS MEDTNER

CLASSIC VERSUS ULTRA-MODERN MUSIC

UNTIL his present visit to America, in 1924, Nicholas Medtner had been little more than a name to many of us on this side of the Atlantic. Occasionally we heard one or two of his compositions played in recital, perhaps by one of his compatriots—Rachmaninoff, Prokofieff or Moiseiwitsch—or his name had been included in accounts of the modern school of Russian composers. But that was about all. This year he is with us, a present personality, and has proved himself, besides being a modern composer, to be an exceptionally fine pianist. His début with the Philadelphia Orchestra was an event of musical significance, as it introduced the artist to this country in the double light of composer and executant. It may be added that he shone brightly in both.

It may be of interest to set down a few facts concerning the career of this distinguished musician from Russia. He was born in Moscow, in

1879, and early showed signs of exceptional musical talent. Entering the Moscow Conservatoire in 1891, he was fortunate in being placed in the hands of Safonoff, whose splendid training has given Russia some excellent pianists, among them Rachmaninoff and Scriabine, both of whom, like Medtner, developed a high order of interpretative power.

Medtner remained at the Conservatoire till 1900—about nine years—and finished his course with high honors. Shortly afterward he won the coveted Rubinstein prize for piano playing in Vienna. Several years were now spent in tours throughout Russia and Germany, as a pianist. In 1909, the artist was appointed Professor of Piano in the Conservatory of Moscow, a position he continued to hold—with the exception of a year or two devoted entirely to composition—till 1921. Since 1922, Medtner has made his home in Berlin.

These are the outstanding facts of his life and career. But what of the man himself? Should one succeed in passing the formal barriers behind which every artist of note is entrenched, one will meet a very quiet gentleman, of most serious mien. He impresses one as a man entirely modest and quite unwilling to talk about himself, his doings or achievements. Not only so, but he seems to consider it well-nigh unseemly to give any personal judgment on the work he has accomplished, either as composer or pianist. Let the world do that. For himself it is artistic satisfaction enough to express himself through both mediums.

In a talk with the composer-pianist, in regard to technical material for piano study, he expressed himself emphatically in favor of technical practise outside of pieces.

"You will find every worthwhile pianist must do special technical work beyond what is found in pieces," he remarked. "It is a necessity for the artist, in order to keep his playing mechanism in good condition. Not only scales and arpeggios, chords and octaves and mechanical forms can be used, but many stretching and gymnastic exercises are needed." As he spoke he glanced down at his own hands, shapely and supple, but rather small, and doubtless thought of the constant training which had been necessary to develop and render them serviceable and responsive.

"What composers do I esteem most highly? Personally, I prefer the music of Beethoven and Chopin—that is to say, from the pianist's point of view. Naturally, I admire all the great ones, from Bach to Wagner. Bach's music is surely a treasure-trove for the pianist. What a wealth of ideas! What invention—what true feeling! I am also very fond of the old masters of Bach's time and a little later, especially Scarlatti. Then there is Schumann, whose compositions I greatly esteem and love. As for Brahms, on the other hand, I play very little of his music. It does not seem pianistic to my sense, or perhaps I should rather say it does not appeal to me. I feel he is much greater in his chamber music, his fine symphonies and other orchestral compositions—yes, and in his songs also—than he is for the piano. Of Franz Liszt, too, I play very little, probably because his music does not make a strong appeal to me."

Speaking of ultra-modernism in music and the following it has attracted, Medtner continued:

"With so-called ultra-modern music I have absolutely no sympathy. It seems to me a thing apart, not to be mentioned in the same sentence with true, legitimate musical art. I find absolutely nothing in it; it says nothing to me— nothing but discord. I am not a modernist, you see. This does not mean unwillingness to listen to what the moderns have to say. I do listen and honestly try to find something in it to arouse feeling and sympathy, but always fail to find these or anything at all that appeals. It all seems so useless and futile, both for the composer to spend his time with and the hearer to attend and listen.

"Why cannot modern music keep to some sort of form? Why cannot it express beauty instead of ugliness? But it seems as though ugliness and distortion were the prime factors of the music of today. It should not render music less beautiful and vital because it obeys laws of harmony and rhythm. Fortunately for the cause of art, there are a few composers today who realize this, and who seek to make music beautiful and valued for itself. Rachmaninoff is one of these. His is the sort of modern music I admire, and he is the foremost Russian composer we have today."

STYLE IN COMPOSITION

It has been said of Medtner that his creative work bears evidence of deep personal feeling and a reverence for purity of form unmatched by the work of any other living creative artist. The spirit of his music is that of the great romanticists of the past, reinforced by modern thought— modern aims and ideas. While he is more romantic than his predecessors, yet in comparison with such moderns as Scriabine and Stravinsky, he is really a classicist. He has invented musical art-forms that are designed for his own use and might fail to suit the ideas of other composers. He has sought and found musical expression for his own emotions, for his own experiences in life. And he is not content to express these in the form and shape which other and earlier musicians have used, but has evolved his own idiom. Thus his pieces take on specialties, in order to embody his own peculiar moods and feelings.

MUSIC FOR PIANO

Up to now Medtner has written a goodly number of piano pieces, including a piano Concerto, many songs, a Sonata and three Nocturnes for piano and violin. Among the piano pieces are the Eight Mood Pictures, Op. 1. Then comes a fine Sonata, Op. 5. Three Sonatas (Sonaten Triaden) in A flat, D minor and C major, Op. 11; Sonata in G minor, Op. 22; two Sonatas, Op. 25; Sonata Ballade, Op. 27. Numerous smaller pieces are also included in the list.

At his first recital in New York, the composer played nine of his own compositions. There were six "Maerchen," taken from Ops. 26, 34, 14, 20 and 19. They really seemed pictures of moods, now bright, now somewhat sad—gay and triste by turns. After these followed three Dances, from *Forgotten Motives*, Ops. 38 and 40.

The C minor piano Concerto, with which

Medtner introduced himself to America, was composed in 1918, and performed in Moscow the same year, at a concert conducted by Koussevitzky. The work consists of one movement and is an elaboration of the classical sonata form. The composer, describing his work, said in part:

"Broadly speaking, the work consists of two chief themes, developed in a series of Variations with a Recapitulation. The principal theme is announced by the violins, following three measures of stormy introduction by the piano. The second theme is sung by the 'cellos, against an ascending passage of chords and octaves for the piano. As a subsidiary theme, there is a rhapsodic cantilena by the piano. It is echoed by a solo horn, after which the piano continues it for fifteen measures. This is developed, together with the two chief themes, and followed by a cadenza for the piano.

"After this the Variations are begun by muted 'cellos. There are nine Variations, followed by the Recapitulation. The Coda begins softly, combining the two chief themes, and there is a brilliant close in C major."

MEDTNER AS PIANIST

The pianist Medtner impresses one as a very serious, thoughtful artist, whose aim is to apprehend the exact meaning of the composer he is interpreting, and to transmit this meaning to the listener. He has an ample technic, a musical touch, and much variety of tone, in both powerful and delicate passages. He plays with vigor and animation, though his desire always appears to be to express the meaning of the music. As one would naturally expect from such a mentality, there is no seeking for spectacular effects, no desire for display, either in personal appearance, manner, or performance. Just a quiet gentle-man, who is artist to his finger-tips, and who desires to give the results, in his playing and interpretation, of a lifetime of serious, earnest study, of devotion to the highest ideals of art for the love of art; in short, one of the true musicians of his day and generation.

XV

MME. OLGA SAMAROFF

PIANISTIC PROBLEMS

OLGA SAMAROFF is a well-known figure in the pianistic world. In spite of her Russian name, she is an American. Early showing signs of musical gifts, she first studied music at home, then in Paris, with Marmontel and Widor, and afterward was the first American woman to be admitted to the piano classes of Delabord at the Conservatoire. Later she went to Jedliczka in Berlin. Her American début was made in New York with the New York Symphony Orchestra in 1905. Since then Mme. Samaroff has played in many concerts and recitals all over the world.

In response to my questions in regard to pianistic problems, the pianist answered as follows:

"The questions you ask, which involve piano training and development, tone production, different varieties of touch, how to acquire power, delicacy and velocity, how to memorize, and use of metronome, cover such a vast field that one

146

MME. OLGA SAMAROFF

could almost write a book on each subject. I will try to touch lightly on them all.

STUDY THE PUPIL

"It seems to me that about the greatest problem confronting the teacher is to know how to treat his pupil individually. I have so often seen the same method succeed wonderfully with one pupil and fail dismally with another. In a particular case I have in mind, both pupils were musical, and there was not enough difference in intelligence, application and general qualities to account for the enormous difference in results. I believe the difference was more a psychological one than anything else. One must both encourage a pupil and at the same time develop a very stern self-criticism in him that will preclude any possibility of the self-satisfaction which stops all advance. It seems to me psychology plays an enormous part in the study of the piano, as in the study of most things. One great fault with much of the technical training given is that the pupil does not realize exactly—with the utmost distinctness—just why he is doing a certain kind of work, or what results he expects to obtain from it. This is particularly true if teachers take the technical Études of Clementi, Czerny, Pischna, and others, and use them automatically, without making the pupil study deeply into the real problems confronting him and the exact value of the given technical material for overcoming them. With the proper mental attitude, right physical conditions and proper amount of work, every ordinarily intelligent person ought to be able to acquire the necessary piano technic. It is evident that the best way to develop piano technic is to examine closely into the various kinds of finger and wrist work required, select the exercises which seem, from an intellectual standpoint, the most apt to produce results, and then work on till one has obtained them.

TONE PRODUCTION

"Tone production is not nearly so much a question of touch as of *hearing*. If a student has that acute sense of musical hearing which enables him to distinguish the finest gradations of tone (and this quality is a natural and inborn one), he will instinctively touch the key in such a way as to produce the quality of tone which his instinct leads him to desire. It seems to me very difficult to develop tone production in a purely intellectual way. Of all the qualities which go to make up piano playing, this is the one most necessarily instinctive. If the teacher has a pupil with a thin, anemic tone, he can gradually improve it by requiring more pressure, loose hand, arm and so on. But I doubt if any player, not naturally gifted with a discriminating sense of sound, can acquire a really beautiful tone production.

DELICACY AND VELOCITY

"Delicacy and velocity both come from strength and complete muscular control. Fingers, hands and arms must first acquire strength. The delicacy born of strength comes naturally when strength is once there. Velocity is largely a mental quality. If one's thoughts work quickly and have proper control over one's hands and fingers, the principle of velocity will present no difficulty. To a player with a sluggish mind, no amount of muscular practise is going to produce velocity until thought has grasped the concept of swiftness.

MEMORIZING

"In regard to memorizing, I will only speak briefly. I always memorize a composition in sections. To give an example: Suppose we take a passage of eight measures. I practise this until it is committed to memory. Proceeding to practise the following passage, I always begin, not at the beginning of the second eight measures, but two or three measures back. In this way the joining-on measure between passage one and passage two gets double practise, and one has, so to speak, a cue before every passage, which greatly aids in sureness.

THE METRONOME

"In my own work, I have limited the use of the metronome entirely to determining the tempo of a composition—that is to say, if a metronome-mark has been placed there by the composer. Even if this is the case, however, one often finds it impossible to follow given directions. As for working with the metronome otherwise, I cannot imagine it to be a very good thing, as it might lead pupils to rely on an artificial support in rhythmic movement, whereas they should develop their own sense of rhythm unaided. However, it may be that teachers of great experience have found other good uses for the metronome.

THE PEDALS

"One of the enormously important things in piano playing is the pedal. A volume could be written on the pedals alone; that is, on their importance and on the wonderful results obtained by artistic pedaling. There again, pedaling is one of those instinctive things which seems to baffle both teacher and student. I tried recently, after hearing a young pianist play, who had spoiled everything with a bad use of pedals, to write out the pedaling, in the most minute way, for an entire composition, even giving the half-pedals—that is to say, a pedal raised only half-way, to reduce sonority in certain places. The young pianist in question went home and studied the piece with most praiseworthy diligence. The result was almost comical in its stiffness and pedantry. Although perfectly correct, it did not in the least give the effects I had expected. On seating myself at the piano and looking over my pedal markings, I found the reason. It was because I did not pedal the same way the second time; in fact, I found that I did not pedal twice in exactly the same way. I discovered that the degree of sonority employed made countless changes in the duration of the pedal and the exact point of releasing it. So finally I was obliged to give up my demonstration for the young pianist in question. To me pedaling has always been as natural as breathing, and I believe it must be so to most pianists. Of course, the general rules for putting down the pedal after depressing a key or chord and taking it up before changing to the next chord are known to practically all music students and are very gen-

erally applied. But the really wonderful effects
of pedaling, which go far beyond these general
rules, are too subtle to be caught. My advice to
piano students in this, as in the case of tone production, is to *listen for yourselves.* If you have
natural gifts, which, after all, are so very necessary to artistic work on the piano, they will,
through listening and thinking, find the right
way."

THE BEETHOVEN SONATAS

A gifted American has just accomplished a
wonderful feat, demonstrating both memory and
musicianship. To play the entire thirty-two
Sonatas of Beethoven has never before been attempted in America by a native artist. We are
proud to recognize the ability of our country-
woman, who has the talent, courage and perseverance to bring the idea to a successful
fulfillment. This is indeed a Beethoven year,
and Mme. Samaroff has been able to make the
largest contribution of any single artist towards
the celebration of the master's memory.

In performing these beautiful works, Mme.
Samaroff is well equipped for the task. She
possesses reliable technic, the utmost clarity of
touch, a commendable command of dynamics.

She holds up the work she is playing before the listener as though it were a picture, reproduced in every detail. It is as though one saw the work reflected in a mirror, so exact is every part. Those who followed, book in hand, could not detect a wrong note anywhere. This surety of reproduction by the pianist is one of her charms; you feel absolute security as you listen, for you feel there is no danger of a slip.

And the controlling memory which is able to reproduce these great works, one after another —what of that? This is what I wanted especially to ask Mme. Samaroff; for this, I am sure, will interest every pianist and teacher. Not until eight recitals—into which she had arranged the Sonatas—were over, was an hour found in which we could discuss the absorbing topic of how she prepared her Sonata programs. As we sat in the beautiful French apartment of the residence where she was stopping, while she described her manner of working and studying, it seemed an easy task to memorize Beethoven's Sonatas, and one wondered why more students and players do not make a study of these great works.

"First of all," began Mme. Samaroff, "I think one must have a retentive memory to start with. It has always been easy for me to memorize. If I take up a piece of music and look it through a couple of times, I can often remember it without really learning it.

"I have always been exceedingly fond of Beethoven's music, but, though I was somewhat familiar with all the Sonatas in a general way, I had not really studied more than seven or eight of them, but those I knew backward as well as forward. This, then, was my foundation; of course I had no idea I should ever do them in recital.

"I think Mr. Gabrilowitsch is really the source of my inspiration to make a more complete study of this music. In the summertime, at Seal Harbor, he would often come into our home and play the Sonatas for us. In this way I heard them frequently and was fired with a desire to do them myself.

TIME REQUIRED

"It may surprise you to know it has not taken the great amount of time to prepare them that you suppose. About three years ago I decided on the plan. But you know an artist cannot use the winter months for study of new material, for one's time must be devoted to concert work. It is only the summer that can be counted on, three or four months at most. In that short period one must accomplish a year's work. I was in

Europe last summer and played at the Mahler
Festival and in other places. This interrupted
the work somewhat, so that altogether I have not
given more than seven or eight months to close
study.

THE UNDERSTANDING

"I feel that memorizing is the smallest part of
the work. It is the understanding of form and
structure, the meaning of the music that is to be
interpreted, the analyzing of each part in detail,
the bringing out prominent parts, subduing
others, making all a complete whole—a perfect
picture. That is where deep thought and study
are necessary. Some parts or movements are
much more difficult to master, technically, but
easier to remember than others. The Waldstein,
Op. 53, is quite easy to remember, while the
shorter one, Op. 54, presents unexpected difficulties.

THE MEMORIZING

"In committing to memory I have, of course,
my own little devices for contrasting themes or
passages—the likes and unlikenesses, and other
things that help fix the composition in mind. I
do not visualize the page, as though I saw it before me, as some players do. The ear plays the

biggest part; I remember through the ear. I hear it all mentally, not thinking ahead, or expecting what is coming—because that divides the attention, but just hearing the music as it unfolds under my fingers. I think there is a good deal of virtue in having finger memory, too. If you know the piece well enough and have played it long enough, the fingers find the keys themselves. And sometimes you can just leave them to do it, while you let up the tension, as it were, sit back and let the music pour forth without care.

"Then there is the thinking through a piece mentally, away from the piano. I can do this sometimes as I walk along the street. Of course, I think it in the same movement and tempo as though I were actually playing it at the piano. This is also ear memory. When committing at first, I often do so away from the instrument, but not always—especially if I am in a hurry. But the ear is the chief factor with me, in any case. That is why I do not care to follow a performance with book or score; this is using both eye and ear, which is apt to confuse the thought. So I prefer to listen and not use eye at the same time.

"I think one should live with a work for some time before venturing to perform it in public—

several months at least. Some artists do not
agree with me, for they often bring out a piece
almost as soon as it is memorized. That is not
my way. That is one reason why, earlier in my
career, I did not do much Beethoven; I felt I
must work on his music much longer; I felt I
was not mature enough.

KEEPING REPERTOIRE IN REVIEW

"How do I keep the Sonatas in review? I
have learned them, they are mine, and can never
be taken from me, for I know them thoroughly.
Naturally, if I am going to play them at a certain
time, I will go over the program very carefully,
to make sure everything is all right, and will,
of course, work over the difficult places, and all
that. If you have a piece of silver, it does not
change its shape, size or chasing and ornament
because it lies a while in a drawer unused. It
may tarnish a little, that is true, but you can
soon rub it up and put it in shape again.

ACQUIRING THE SONATA HABIT

"I have greatly enjoyed this work with the
Sonatas, for some of them, as I said already, were
almost new to me, especially the earlier ones.
And I find that students, and players, often
neglect the early Sonatas. Young people come

to play for me, to get advice about a musical career. Asked about repertoire—well, they have but one Beethoven Sonata, perhaps, along with their Chopin, Liszt and modern music. The Sonata is never earlier than the Pathétique, Op. 13; it is more often the Waldstein or the Appassionata. I think students should become familiar with the earlier works, for they are very beautiful too. They should get the 'Sonata habit,' so to say. It will do them a world of good. When you think of it, the Sonatas of Beethoven contain about every technical problem that can be thought of. That is one reason why I do not practise so-called pure technic outside of pieces; for it has not been necessary while I have been working on the Sonatas.

"The people everywhere seem to be fond of Beethoven's music, and anxious to hear the Sonatas. I have played the complete set of Sonatas in Philadelphia, earlier in the season, and now have done them in New York, while I have given Beethoven programs in other cities. I might add that in Philadelphia, Baltimore, Washington, St. Louis and other cities, where I have played Beethoven recitals, it has been to sold-out houses, proving that there is a growing love in America for the best music and most serious works of the greatest composers.

"Things have opened out quite unexpectedly as a result of this work. People ask me, jestingly, what composer I intend to take up next, and suggest I select Bach, for instance.

"One must always keep at work; for serious work, to the artist, is pure delight."

XVI

ARTUR SCHNABEL

THE WORK OF THE TEACHER

ARTUR SCHNABEL, distinguished pianist and teacher, known to some of our younger American players who have studied with him in Berlin, paid his first visit to America during the season of 1922-1923. Mr. Schnabel had long contemplated coming, but untoward conditions had prevented. We found him a serious, earnest musician, with a very highly developed technic. Schnabel was with Liszt for about nine years. After this period, he made many successful tours through Europe, usually residing in Berlin.

I welcomed the opportunity to confer with so successful a pianist and teacher, on how to handle various types of students.

Starting with a simple question of what to do with weak fingers, the artist spoke long and earnestly on pedagogical subjects.

"I have thought very seriously about the question of how to start a child in music study, or rather piano study. The greatest technical necessity for all players, big and little, is to have a firm third phalange, or nail-joint. There must be no giving in or weakness there. The nail-joint must be like a rock in its firmness. All other joints and hinges may be loose—the knuckles, wrist, arm, elbow, shoulder, yes, and the back, neck and muscles about the jaw, too—all loose and relaxed. But not the nail-joint. That is to be as iron.

"Now, with children that joint is usually very weak, and a teacher has great difficulty in cultivating any firmness at all in it. I have about come to the conclusion that the teacher, at the beginning, must be somewhat lenient in this one particular and not expect or require too much. You may not agree to this, but let me make it quite clear. When the child endeavors to play with firmness in the nail-joint, he will probably stiffen the neck and back, which is detrimental to good tone production. In order to avoid the greater evil, it may be necessary to suffer the lesser one for a time, till small fingers gain a little strength and become somewhat accustomed to depressing the keys.

"Naturally, in my own case, I have no time to give to any players who come to me unprepared. If they have outstanding faults of a technical nature, I give them advice how to correct these, and leave it to them to accomplish. Of course I accept only those who are musically gifted. I teach only a few months in the year, and during the ten lessons I may give a pupil, my whole attention must be focussed on the interpretation, for there is no time to attend to minor technical faults. During the ten lessons the player may bring me ten pieces, one for each lesson. I can hear them but once.

"To return to the beginner. To train a gifted child, or even one not so gifted, much has to be considered. We should not only look after technical development, but the musical development as well. The mental faculties must be trained from all sides. There is the ear to be cultivated in listening. So many pupils think they are studying music; yet all the time they are never trying to listen to it, or what they are doing in it. Then there is sight-reading, which is so often neglected. A certain amount of time daily should be given to this side of the work.

"Writing, or rather, I should say, copying music, is a great aid in musical development. Let the young student spend half an hour a day in copying the Preludes and Fugues from Bach's *Well-tempered Clavichord,* first from the book and later from memory, as he learns to play them. In this way he lays a solid musical foundation.

"The modern player who would master the modern instrument must realize that he has to cultivate the whole body, and not simply the fingers. Body and arm weight must be brought into use to aid the fingers to play with sufficient power and sonority. All the artists of the present day use arm weight constantly. Therefore the young student soon begins, through the practise of simple chords in different positions, to employ this relaxed arm weight. He combines arm freedom with finger development, and so gains quality and sonority of tone.

THE PIANO NOT A SOLO INSTRUMENT

"It is a mistaken idea to consider the piano as a solo instrument. The only strictly solo instrument I can think of is the simple shepherd's pipe, which he blows upon, a single note at a time, to call his sheep. No, our instrument is a string quartet, or a full orchestra, as the case may be. No piano piece is ever written for a single voice; there is always a combination of voices, just as there is in chamber music, or in the orchestra. And do not forget that every note in a worthy composition is of musical value; it belongs to the plan, the scheme; it cannot be ignored or slighted, except to the injury of the whole. This is the wonderful business connected with the study of our art, namely, to set forth each note in its right relation to every other note. All this means the most careful thought, the closest listening, the most studious concentration. Only those who cultivate these qualities, or possess them naturally or intuitively, really succeed in music—that is, succeed in the best sense.

THE PRESENT OUTLOOK

"As we look out on the world today, do we see the young students of music thoroughly grounded in the foundation principles of our art, advancing logically from a solid foundation to highest musicianship? Do we see high ideals of musical art fostered and upheld? Alas, no. On the contrary, we find them commercialized and lowered to suit popular taste. The age is very complex. In a former time there were real amateurs and dilettante, using these terms in the best sense. I mean to say, that in a former time people cultivated the art of music for its own sake and for the pleasure and enjoyment to be derived from it. Such people formed the listeners at musical performances; they were thoroughly familiar with the classics and music of all styles, which the artist would interpret. Between such listeners and the artist there was an invisible bond of sympathy; he felt they could understand him and what he was trying to do. It seems to me this kind of listener has greatly diminished in numbers. I could almost say we have no amateurs, in just that sense, in these days. People do not cultivate our art for their own pleasure and self-improvement, but to make money out of it, to commercialize it, to degrade it to a mere vapid amusement.

"Why have we so few musical amateurs? I am not speaking of America any more than the rest of the world. Why have we?

"For one thing there is no leisure. Where the people of yesterday had ten things to occupy themselves with, people of today have a million. They rush from this to that—here and there—the whole day through. It is business—politics—a little of this or that, and the time slips by, frittered away in a whirlwind of complexities. How can a serious art be studied and enjoyed amid such a mass of varied interests? The many inventions of modern life, too, add to this confusion of interests. The people of yesterday found time to enjoy the landscape on foot. Where is there time today for long walks into the country, or suburbs, to study nature, the wonders of wood, field or sky? If we do go through the country, it is by motor, and at a furious rate.

"I am not saying the world of today is worse than the world of yesterday. I only say it is different. And we must handle it differently. I feel that unless we do so, our art will become anemic, or atrophied, for lack of the clear sunlight and fresh air of well-employed leisure, to study thoroughly, to listen attentively, to concentrate systematically.

"And now a few words more about piano touch and relaxation, even at the risk of repeating myself. As has been said, all players must cultivate firm third joints of the fingers; without this there can be no stability or accuracy. Then there must be finger action. In the beginning there must be a foundation of exact finger movements, from the knuckle-joints. When that has been accomplished, the hand itself plays more and more of a rôle in piano touch. If I have a passage of five notes to play—say from thumb to fifth finger, I do not make up and down movements with hand in stiff position. No, I lead the hand in the direction of the trend of the passage, whether it be up or down. So that one might say the hand plays more than the fingers. The fingers are all of different lengths, and ought to be treated individually. The longer fingers can slide somewhat up or into the key, especially in melody playing. I try to avoid the hammer touch, so-called, and combine more of hand and arm weight with finger stroke and pressure.

"We must also cultivate the condition of relaxation. Every part of the mechanism must be capable of relaxing at any moment. The muscles of neck and back must be loose; arms must not hug the sides of the body, but must be allowed to hang a little away from them. Acquire the sensation of relaxation, by reclining in a lounging chair or on a couch, in order to experience just what the feeling is. Then apply this condition when at the piano.

"I feel that the study of music is one of the greatest any one can pursue. When possible, it ought to be undertaken for the love of the art, and not always with a financial end in view. For myself, I have no wish merely to 'please the public,' if it means lowering a high ideal. Rather educate the public to appreciate and love the highest and best in our art."

Speaking of mechanical records, Mr. Schnabel added:

"The records of musical performances, especially those of piano playing, are noteworthy. But we should not look upon them as a menace to the general study of the piano by young people. Let us rather consider them as aids to spread the knowledge of piano literature and a love of good music. For we will not forget that, no matter how excellent the mechanical record, nothing will ever take the place of playing by hand. No mechanism can usurp the spontaneous outpouring of the individual artist at the keyboard, pouring out his soul in the rapt absorption of his art."

XVII

BENNO MOISEIWITSCH

THE STUDY AND ART OF PIANO PLAYING

At this particular stage in world history, can it be imagined just what would be the emotions of a great artist of the keyboard, on arriving in America on a first visit, with the avowed object of making his art known to an entirely new world? Everything must be novel and strange. To a sensitive, artistic nature the experience is little short of epochal. Doubtless he would like to ask endless questions as to the why and wherefore of things that are different. It may be he wisely refrains at first from asking too many, for in a short time the objects and things about him begin to assume normal relations to each other, and true perspective appears.

I had the privilege of greeting Mr. Moiseiwitsch before he had been on American soil twenty-four hours. He had had a rough, uncomfortable trip, and was as yet hardly recovered from the effect of the inconvenience he had experienced. He was located in agreeable quarters, a little apart from thoroughfares usually frequented by foreign visitors, and in his pleasant sitting-room, with its grand piano standing ready for his hand, we had an intimate talk about the study and art of piano playing.

The young Russian artist meets the visitor with simple, unaffected friendliness, in which there is no posing nor striving for effect. Slender and pliant in figure, with wonderfully supple hands, his dark, expressive face, with its large eyes, reflects a poetical spirit. One feels here is a rare mentality, one which will feel the meaning of the music and will possess ample resources through which to reveal this meaning to the listener.

"I do not care for fireworks in piano playing," he began; "at least I am not that kind of player; I want to get at the meaning of the composition and reveal that; I want to say what is in my heart to say about the music, without bombast of any kind. In short, the virtuosity side of piano playing does not appeal to me. Although, for example, Liszt's music tends to that side of pianism, I am devoted to some of it—to the B minor Sonata in particular, and to some of the transcriptions of songs. A few of the Rhapsodies I do not care so much for, though some others I admire greatly.

BENNO MOISEIWITSCH

THE SUBJECT OF TECHNIC

"You ask me about the technical side of piano study. Technic is a difficult subject to define; it depends so much on correct understanding of conditions—of the *feeling* one experiences while employing the fingers. It is knowing how to use one's hands; it is control. Before I went to Leschetizky, I had never studied technic for itself alone—in fact I had never thought much about the subject. I had always played the piano for the sheer pleasure of playing. But when I went to Vienna I had to get right down to rock bottom, drop all my piece-playing and simply work at technic. For several months I did nothing but that, working with Fraülein Prentner, one of the strictest of the assistant teachers. I studied very hard at that time to master technical principles, conquer my shortcomings and gain the necessary control of the piano and of myself. For control is required by the pianist—he must have it.

"When I at last finished the preparation and began work with the master himself, I found him to be a wonderful teacher. He would often allow the student to play through the composition without interruption, until it was quite finished. Then came the criticism. He seemed to dissect a piece as a botanist picks a flower to pieces. For he had the gift to discover just what was wrong with one's fingers, and could point out the way to correct the student's faults and show him exactly how to get the right results. He would illustrate at his own piano the desired effect, and then show just how it could be attained.

"One of the wonderful things about his teaching—the thing I am most grateful to him for—was the light he threw on the subject of tone color and variety of tonal dynamics. I now began to learn what tone color really meant. That, too, is such a matter of physical feeling and the manner of touching the keys. The size and formation of hand has much to do with the manner in which one handles the keyboard. A master teacher may play a passage and ask the student to repeat it in the same manner. Perhaps one player can do so; another is quite unable to manage it. Why? Often from physical causes. For no two hands are exactly alike; neither is mental ability the same.

TECHNICAL PRACTISE

"When I start the day, I do not begin with a lot of scales and exercises, as so many players do, thus using the precious hours of the morning for mechanical study. No, I desire to enjoy my piano at all times, especially in the early part of the day. I begin with a piece, one that I know; it may be a Prelude and Fugue of Bach, from the *Well-tempered Clavichord*. I play it through, without stopping. If there are places in it which do not go as they should, owing to a certain finger, or fingers, which do not act correctly, I return to these portions, see what the trouble is, and discipline the intractable fingers with improvised exercises. I also take the passages in question and make special studies out of them, using a variety of rhythms, accents and fingerings. Advanced technique should consist largely in making studies from difficult passages in pieces.

SPEAKING OF MEMORIZING

"Another difficult subject is to explain just how one memorizes the music one plays. Each pianist seems to have his own method of committing music to memory. It has always been very easy for me, so perhaps that is why I have no cut-and-dried manner of doing it.

"I generally do memory work at the piano, by playing the piece in sections and studying them out in details. For a concerto I must know the whole orchestral score as well as my solo parts. A little illustration of how quickly I can memorize when obliged to do so, was on the occasion of my playing the Tscherepnine Concerto with Sir Henry Wood's Orchestra in London. They had asked me to play something new, and three modern works had been submitted to me to look over: namely, the aforesaid Concerto, one by Prokofieff, and one other. I preferred the first to either of the others, but the orchestral parts for it were not at hand. As the concert was not to take place for several months, the matter was left in this rather vague way, and I had quite forgotten it, as I was busy with concerts in different parts of the country. Just nine days before the concert was to take place, I happened to read an announcement that I was to play the Tscherepnine Concerto on this occasion. This was a surprise, to say the least. I at once began to work on the Concerto, committed it to memory and played it on the appointed date. It is a work of about eighty pages, with a cadenza of about fifteen pages in length. This Concerto is as yet quite unknown in America, and I hope to play it during my visit here."

At that time doubtless Mr. Moiseiwitsch did not realize the difficulty of bringing out new works which are unknown to orchestras and conductors.

"As to keeping up my repertoire, of course I

go over my pieces very carefully before a recital,
to see that all is well with them. It is interesting
to test them out in my own studio, without re-
ferring to the score, to see how they have been
preserved, and whether I remember them perfectly. When one goes minutely over a composition, one discovers new beauties each time,
new effects which can be made. Yes, I travel
with copies of the pieces I am to play, so that
I can refer to them at any time. The only time
I study the printed page away from the piano
is when I am on the road, between concerts."

The pianist again reverted to his master,
Leschetizky.

"He was a wonderful teacher in so many ways.
He was a great reader of character, and could
appraise the student's mentality with psychological accuracy. For instance, he would hear
the same piece from two players and would teach
it differently to each one of them. Again he was
able to apprehend just the difficulty the student
was laboring under—as I have said—and could
tell one what to do to remove it. On one occasion I was playing the G major Prelude of
Chopin. He seemed satisfied with the performance until I came to the last line, where the
arpeggio passage for two hands occurs. This
did not seem to suit him. Instead of saying, 'No,

that is not good, you must improve it,' as so many masters would do, he simply remarked, 'Why don't you loosen your arms and make an undulating movement as you go up the keyboard?' for he saw I was a little stiff and constrained when playing that ascending passage. The simple remark was a revelation to me. I found I could now render the passage with the utmost ease."

Mr. Moiseiwitsch moved from his chair to the piano and played the Prelude in question (so familiar to all piano students) with a clarity and fluidity of utterance, a variety of tonal color, a freedom of movement, truly ravishing.

"Of course," he said, "one must use care not to overdo this undulating movement, as it might easily be abused."

The artist was much interested to know the inclinations of American audiences in regard to classical and modern music. He expressed his preference for Schumann's music, and has given several entire programs of this master's compositions. "I do not think a large auditorium is suitable for my instrument," he said; "I would prefer to play in smaller spaces; if I could have my way, I would play in a room of this size. I prefer intimate surroundings, not a great stage and the big spaces of a vast concert hall."

In this regard, Mr. Moiseiwitsch agrees with Chopin, who was averse to exhibiting his delicate art to great audiences. And, indeed, the Russian artist appears to have many points of resemblance to the Polish master. One cannot help feeling he must also be—as he later proved himself—"a poet of the piano."

The Russian pianist has just completed a second visit to America. When he came to us three years ago, we found him a cultured musician who played both classic and modern music with technical command and poetic insight. At his single recital in New York on this second visit, the critics found he had made tremendous strides in absolute command of all pianistic resources; in short that he had returned "a digital and technical giant—a real virtuoso."

"What is the difference between an artist and a virtuoso—or what is the true meaning of virtuoso?" I put the question to Mr. Moiseiwitsch at our little conference, a day or two after his recital.

"I hardly know how to define the term *virtuoso*," he answered thoughtfully. "The word means something out of the ordinary, something unusual, dazzling, magical, to attract the crowd. This attracting force is liable to be focused on technic; for supreme agility in manipulating the keyboard is what first impresses the superficial. This may, or may not, be quite apart from the meaning of the music. The musical and emotional import of the composition is what should concern the interpreter, and that is the only side which interests me.

"How have I gained increased facility? A musician must continue to grow, if he keeps on working. I know I have gained in command of my instrument, in the greater understanding of the means used to obtain pianistic effects, and in control of myself and my resources.

TECHNIC

"Naturally one must have some daily technical routine, and must in time discover what technical forms are best for him, and go to the root of the matter most completely and quickly. As he advances in absolute control and mastery, technical tasks become effortless, a part of himself, and he seeks more and more to voice the higher, the spiritual, meaning of the music he plays.

"Some of the critics have mentioned velocity. Well, why should there not be velocity, if it does not interfere with form and shape?" Turning to the keyboard, the artist illustrated convincingly. "Suppose I play Chopin's Étude on the Black Keys, like this, at a moderately quick tempo. Then suppose I play it now much faster; there is no harm in this, *if* I keep everything clear and well balanced. The Bach Chromatic Fantaisie can start off at a lively pace; later it becomes more introspective and dreamy. It is a rhapsody all through. And then the wonderful Fugue! There seems to be a genuine Bach revival going on; we see evidences of it on all sides, even to entire Bach programs being played.

PEDALING

"One very important factor in piano playing —one that is often much neglected—is pedaling. The pedals are as important as the fingers; we have the hands, the feet, the head, with which to make music. The third pedal? No, I never use it. I really see no use for it at all, for I can make all the effects I need with the two pedals. I make great use of the left, the so-called soft pedal, combining it with the damper pedal, even in passages that are marked *forte;* it creates shimmering effects of color when used with the so-called loud pedal.

BRAHMS

"Yes, I play much Brahms—of course, the Handel Variations, though I omit a very few of them, and many of the shorter pieces. No, I do not play the Variations on a Schumann Theme. I am now making a record of the Brahms Valses, from which I select about ten or so, and arrange them in a different order from that found in the printed copy. Naturally, I try to select the most characteristic ones. Many are charming and I do not consider it does them any harm to be rearranged.

MODERN MUSIC

"Do I play modern music? I only care to learn what is worth while, what appeals to me as having something to say, as having vitality and meaning. From this viewpoint it doesn't matter whether the music is new or old. Some modern compositions are interesting. You mention the Sonata by Frank Bridge, which Myra Hess played at her recital here. I have heard her do it in London. It is not a work to attract the listener at first hearing. As I have heard it several times, I begin to be somewhat attracted to it. I think she is very brave to play it here, when she must realize it would not *take* at one hearing. It would be unwise, too, to attempt to play it from memory, since one would not use the work often enough to compensate for the time it would consume to commit it.

A PROGRAM OF ÉTUDES

"I have in mind a program made up entirely of Études, which I hope to bring out here. Such a program would consist largely of the Twenty-four Études of Chopin, entire. I don't think they have been played here as a complete whole. But I should not play them in the order they appear in the book. I would begin and end with those originally placed first and last, but others would be arranged differently. I have given much thought to placing them according to type and meaning. Of course these pieces are not studies at all, in any sense, but wonderful works of art, compositions of the highest order. By constant study new beauties are revealed, new ways of interpretation, new atmosphere and tonal coloring.

"Take the Étude in A minor, Number 2, for instance. If I play the right hand like this" (illustrating) "and slightly stress the first sixteenth note in each group of four, a little melody is developed, as you see. It gives variety and meaning to the ascending and descending passages, like a faint pattern in the web of tone weaving. Whenever we can discover a melodic voice, it is our privilege to reveal and bring it out.

"My program of Études can begin with the

Études Symphoniques of Schumann—again a
set of pieces, études only in name. After these
I would place a few of the Liszt Études, the
Gnomenreigen, Waldesrauschen, Étude in D
flat, and a couple of others. I do not want to
make the list too long; the Chopin pieces require
an hour and five minutes to play, the Schumann
about twenty minutes; I would not weary the
listener."

XVIII

MITJA NIKISCH

MEMORIZING THROUGH THE MIND'S EYE

THE name Arthur Nikisch was almost as well
known in America as in Europe, during the last
decade. It belonged to a thoroughly trained
musician, active in several fields of musical art.
As a youth, Arthur Nikisch graduated from
the Vienna Conservatory with prizes for violin
playing and for the composition of a string-
sextet. While still a student, he had the honor
of playing among the first violins, under Wagner, at the laying of the corner-stone of the Festival Theater at Baireuth. Besides being a
composer and violinist, he became an excellent
pianist. Together with these gifts was that of
conducting, by which he was known the world
over.

Engaged as conductor by various great orchestras in Europe, he was finally secured by the
Boston Symphony Orchestra, and held the post
for several years. After returning to Europe,
he conducted the London Philharmonic and

London Symphony Orchestras, making, later, an American tour with the latter orchestra of eighty-five players.

Nikisch was a conductor of the widest sympathies, penetrating insight and extraordinary magnetism; he conducted the most intricate music without score.

It is not at all surprising that when Mitja Nikisch, the son of so distinguished a musician, came before American audiences as a pianist, on his first concert tour, he should be welcomed with interest, even enthusiasm.

It has been said of Mitja Nikisch that he is worthy the great name he bears. It has been indeed a test for the young musician to come, almost unheralded, to a new country and establish such a place for himself as he has done, almost from the start. He has been heard in New York, in recital and with four of the leading orchestras. He also played with the Boston Symphony and gave recitals there and in other large cities. At every appearance he proved himself a serious, capable artist, and one able to fill his playing and his music with the glow of youthful ardor and enthusiasm.

He produces a beautiful tone on the piano, especially in cantilena passages, because he understands and employs the principle of relaxed arm weight. If his excessive movements at times trouble the critics, let them lay the fact to boyish exuberance, which time will mellow. But if exaggerated motion still distracts, let them rather not look but listen to those rich, singing tones, those clear, even scales, smooth arpeggios and robust chords, and thus get the full effect the artist strives to convey.

I have heard the young artist in both recital and with orchestra; I have had several conferences with him about his art, and have always found him, when music is concerned, sincere, unaffected and simple-hearted. There have been trying moments too, as on one occasion, when he must play at a Bagby Musical Morning after an all-night journey from the West. But he has been equal to every emergency. Off duty, as it were, and in moments of relaxation, the charm of youthful eagerness predominates. He seems to enjoy each moment as it comes, and to be ready for each experience. A musical nature that has already achieved much and is brimming with potentialities for the future.

In discussing his work and career, Mitja Nikisch said:

"I began music study at the age of five and a half, and did a little with both piano and violin. My father taught me in the beginning, but he had not the time to continue, as he was so often away from home and always so occupied. After a while I dropped the violin and devoted myself to the piano. At nine I entered the Conservatory at Leipsic, my native city, and became a pupil of Teichmüller. I am sure he is about the greatest teacher in Europe today, for he is still teaching. I enjoyed both class and private instruction with him and found him a wonderful master.

TECHNICAL TRAINING

"As to technical training, it is difficult, nay, almost impossible, to give any rules. Of course foundational principles are the same in every case, but their application and the material used must necessarily vary with each student. This cannot be avoided since each pupil is different, and no two hands are alike. I used many technical forms to acquire facility. There is the Russian Hanon, and others of that school; the French Ducasse, and the German Tausig Daily Studies, the Technics by Biel and Clementi's *Gradus*.

"Outside of the material mentioned, I do much practise of pure technic—scales, always scales, arpeggios, trills and octaves. One must do these things, first to build up a dependable technic and then to preserve and improve it. I also invent many technical forms myself, to fit my needs.

AS TO PIANO PRACTISE

"When I am not in the railway-train, traveling over the country, but am stationary somewhere, I practise four or five hours a day. Then in the summer, when I am free, I practise even more. When at work at the piano, I do not use full power—that is too fatiguing—only half power. And I do much slow playing, using speed only at times. If you ask how I know the amount of power to use in performing a composition in public, I may say I *feel* the effects I want—I *think* them. It is intuition, or inspiration, if you will. One must leave something to the imagination, to the influence of time, place, occasion and surroundings; it cannot always be cut-and-dried, you know.

"It is true the critics took exception to my first American program. I thought I would give something popular, so to say, when I chose the Bach Chromatic Fantasy and Fugue, Beethoven's Appassionata, Liszt's *Love Dream* and Twelfth Rhapsodie. Those are pieces one has heard many times; they are familiar and many students attempt to play them. You see I made it easy for listeners to hear and follow such a program. Later on I shall make a program much more difficult to understand, because I shall choose little-known works, and some Russian modern music.

"You think it was something of a feat to play the Liszt A minor Concerto one day and the Brahms Concerto Number One the next. Yes, both are difficult works, especially the Brahms, and neither is played very often. I am very fond of the Brahms Concerto, and only wish I might have heard the master play it. But, alas, he passed away in 1897, if I remember rightly, and I was born in 1900.

ON MEMORIZING

"Perhaps I have not thought definitely enough as to just how I really do memorize my music. It seems to come to me almost unconsciously after studying the piece, and I suddenly realize I know it, without the need of the printed page. I can say this, however, that I visualize the notes and signs on the printed page, and can really see them before me as I play. I believe that is the most reliable way to learn and retain the notes of a composition. Of course I hear the tones also, so, in fact, I both see and hear them at the same time. Yes, I can memorize away from the keyboard when necessity requires.

THE FEAR OF PUBLIC PLAYING

"It is really sad that there should be such fear about playing from memory; this attacks all kinds of artists. If it could just be done away with—wiped out—what a boon for us all! Some suffer from the fear much more than others. One of the greatest pianists of any time—Anton Rubinstein—was a prey to fear in the most severe form. I have heard my father tell about going to his dressing-room before a concert, and finding him in a high state of nervous excitement. To try and calm himself and become benumbed to this condition, he would be smoking one cigar after another in rapid succession. The air would be so thick that one could hardly distinguish the great artist for the smoke. He died of excessive smoking, you know. The fear that memory would play him false would affect him in unexpected moments: even in a Chopin nocturne—can one fancy it?—he would go to pieces

ORCHESTRAL REPERTOIRE

"I have had great opportunity to play with orchestra, especially under my father's baton. I made my début with him in Leipsic, playing the

Brahms Concerto No. 1. It was called quite a feat, then, for a boy of seventeen to attempt this difficult work. It is indeed one of the most difficult as well as one of the most beautiful of concertos. I have quite a goodly number of concertos in my repertoire. Of Beethoven I play the third, fourth and fifth Concertos, the Schumann in A minor, the two by Chopin, and the two by Liszt. The Saint-Saens in G minor I have not done; so many players do it that it seems unnecessary to add another to the list. None of the five Rubinstein concertos seems to attract me particularly. The D minor is a graceful piece, and it is possible I may take it up a little later. The next concerto I expect to undertake will be Brahms' Second.

"I have played often under my father's direction, perhaps sixty concerts in all. These were given in Germany, Holland, Belgium, England and South America, where we toured together in 1921. Here we were very active, giving thirteen concerts in eighteen days. In a few concerts we played music for two pianos, but my father was so rushed that there was little or no time to prepare. I believe we only gave about six of such concerts in all. But it was in Germany where we played the recitals for two pianos—Leipsic, Dresden, Berlin and other German cities.

RECITALS FOR TWO PIANOS

"Our two-piano recital program was generally made up of three numbers. The first, a Concerto by Bach, arranged for two instruments by Reger. This has an accompaniment for strings, but we played it without, as this addition is optional. Next we played the Schumann Andante and Variations, Op. 46, and, as a close, the Sinding Variations, which are very beautiful. Between these ensemble numbers I played two groups of piano solos.

"My father was a remarkable pianist, and kept up his practise as well as it was possible to do in the face of all the orchestral rehearsals he was obliged to hold. He even tried to do a little violin study each day, if only for half an hour, because he loved both instruments and their music. Once in America, he gave a piano recital. I have forgotten in what city it was—my mother has told me of it.

"I have already mentioned Teichmüller; he was my regular piano teacher and I really received all my training through him. The classes met twice a week, sometimes even three times. They began at ten in the morning and lasted till one, or even longer. The master did not play to us at all; we each played what we had prepared

—always from memory of course. He is really a marvelous teacher in the manner in which he can illumine the music and at the same time show us how to do it. As I said, I had private lessons with him also.

PRESENT-DAY MUSIC

"About present-day music, I don't do the ultra-modern things anyway, unless Scriabine belongs to that list. I am familiar with his ten sonatas; each one of them seems to me a gem. I have looked a little into American music, especially the compositions of MacDowell and his fine sonatas, and may include some of these in my repertoire.

"I have made a partial tour of America this time, and hope to make a longer one when I come again. America is the greatest country to live in these days. I feel very much at home here already, for people have been more than kind to me and to my art."

XIX

MYRA HESS

GLIMPSES OF PRESENT-DAY PIANO STUDY

Myra Hess is spoken of as an English pianist. As a matter of fact her parents were German, though her rich coloring gives one the impression of an Oriental. She is rather slight of figure and one sometimes wonders where the power she occasionally employs comes from. It is well known, however, that when conditions are correct, power can be expressed by simple means and through slight physique.

Miss Hess retires into the background when the subject of personal methods of study or of piano mastery is brought up. She is not anxious to talk about herself, or her particular ways of doing things. "It is so difficult," she says, "to put into words the ways and means one uses to acquire what one seeks. Words are often misleading, and do not express just the shade of thought one desires to give.

"To begin with, I have had a wonderful teacher in Mr. Tobias Matthay, of London. He is such a thorough musician, from every point of view. He sees the subject from all sides, and is so broad and comprehensive in his attitude toward all forms of art. I was placed under his guidance when I was thirteen, and he has trained me entirely ever since. I feel I owe everything to him. I am afraid he spoils me when he speaks so well of me, as he has in the letter you have mentioned. But I always appreciate it very deeply.

FORM AND SHAPE

"When I take up a new work, I try to see it from all sides. By this I mean that I study out the harmony, the chord and key progressions, the technical requirements, then the meaning and necessary interpretation. Some players go about the work in quite a different way. Perhaps they take up first the technical side and make an exhaustive study of that, or they may work a great deal each hand alone, learning each one straight through. The fact is, different pieces ought to be treated differently, each in its own way. In a composition where technical problems predominate, one must of necessity give more attention to that.

"How does one arrive at the understanding of Form and Shape? Through analyzing the com-

Yours sincerely
Myra Hess

position, finding the phrases and half-phrases, and keeping those patterns intact, that is to say, not breaking them up. The phrase is the basis of musical meaning and content, the backbone, as it were, of music itself. Very much has been written about musical form, but very little about its shape, which is just as important. To understand and explain the shape, we must go back to the phrase, and preserve its melodic line.

BALANCE AND PROPORTION

"In regard to balance, I would say that, to attain an understanding of corréct balance in a composition, we should first learn what phrases are more important than others. These are to be brought forward into higher relief, while less important ones drop back into the shadow. A correct comprehension of the phrase and its meaning enables the player to balance all parts artistically. Then there is the balance of tonal values and dynamics, which is an equally fascinating study.

"Again, one of the most important points in the interpretation of a piece is the idea of Proportion, which really means a just balance of all parts and their relation to each other. Matthay is such an authority on this subject. How seldom young players have any exact idea or definite plan for proportion and for balance in their playing! They may produce the tones correctly, may have a good technic and get over the keys quite fluently, in fact; but the meaning of the music they endeavor to interpret lies beyond their grasp, often for lack of any conception of the significance of Proportion, Balance and Shape. Each one of these terms carries a world of meaning with it, as every one knows who has studied at all into the subject. Mr. Matthay gives unceasing care and attention to these things.

"Of what use are correct notes when the form and shape of the phrase are all out of gear? Inexperienced students who accent, phrase, increase and diminish the tone, hurry or retard the tempo in wrong places, disturb the proportion and shape of what they play, and by so doing often miss entirely the meaning of the composition they attempt to interpret. If one does not mentally understand what one is trying to do, one can never really do it. For it is the mind that does the work always. If these subjects of which we have been speaking were more emphasized in teaching, or if teachers had greater knowledge of them, there would be more artistic players in the world, which is a self-evident truism after all," added the pianist with a smile.

MEMORIZING

"How do I memorize? Fortunately, I am blest naturally with an excellent memory, and after I have made a careful study of the piece, noting the points we have dwelt upon, I nearly know it already, without giving special attention to that side of the work. As is well known, there are three kinds of memory training: that of the eye, the ear and the fingers. Although I use all three, I depend, I think, more on the first than on either of the others. I can really see the printed page before me, mentally, and can actually read it as I play, just as though it were on the music-desk before my eyes. There have been times of great stress, when I was mentally agitated and could neither see the notes before me nor even hear them, yet my fingers would go on and continue to play of themselves. Can you imagine it? This fact only proves that one must have keyboard memory as well as both the other kinds. As I seem to depend more frequently on visual memory, I do not like to be long away from the notes of my repertoire, for I must refresh my memory with frequent references to them. Of course I can, and often do, work away from the keyboard, when analyzing and committing to memory.

HOW TO GAIN BOTH POWER AND DELICACY

"I do not practise in any special way for the purpose of gaining power. If tone production is legitimate and correct, one can command the necessary power the moment it is needed. Power is a matter of relaxation; it is not force alone, nor is it only muscular; it is nervous control as well. And thus it is a mental concept, a mental force. If one is able to play softly, with beautiful quality of tone, one should be able to give out a *forte* or *fortissimo* when necessary. Articulation that is soft and at the same time clear, is more difficult to achieve than mere loud playing. It seems to me that the player who has clearness and delicacy, together with good tone, will naturally have necessary power.

"As for using full power during practise, it is something I seldom do. Indeed, it seems to me quite wrong. Especially is it injurious to the ear. One cannot continually listen to such a din, without its deleterious effect on ears and nerves.

THE CLASSICS

"Yes, I play much old classic music. On the modern grand piano, of course, one loses the tinkling quality of tone obtained from old instruments, but something of the effect is preserved by playing lightly and using the pedal sparingly. I want my classics unadulterated, and always prefer to use the original editions rather than those that have been 'edited' or improved upon. I am especially fond of Bach, and there is so much of him! I should like to take a year off, sometime, and do the whole two books of the Preludes and Fugues; it would be great fun! Yes, I would always play the Fugue corresponding to the Prelude. I cannot imagine playing the Prelude alone: it would be like having a body without feet.

"While I love Bach, I am extremely fond of the Scarlatti music, as well as pieces by the old French classicists, Rameau, Lully, and the rest. This music is being 'rediscovered,' as it were, in these days. Players are delving into these forgotten riches and bringing forth fascinating things. I have put some of these little-known pieces of old masters on my programs this season, and intend to prepare many more for use next year. Such compositions seem more modern now than one would imagine, especially when played on our present-day grands.

MODERN PIANO MUSIC

"Do not think that I give myself over to the charms of old music to the exclusion of the new.

I play much Debussy, Ravel, and other French music, not forgetting modern Russian. I also want to bring out and make familiar to American audiences some up-to-date British music—pieces by Arnold Bax, Delius, Bridge, and others. A humorous little incident, anent modern music, happened recently. I was engaged to play a program for a club, and was asked to make my scheme very modern. I did so, choosing largely from the music of Debussy, Ravel, Scriabine and the like. I imagined it might be too stiff for them. Can you guess my surprise when it was returned to me with the request that I give them something much more modern than that! So I had to set to work on the very latest things obtainable.

"Yes, I am somewhat familiar with the Mac-Dowell Sonatas. Besides being modern, they are very interesting works in the sonata form. While I like certain parts and movements in each one immensely, I do not find the complete work, as a whole, exactly adapted to public performance; the interest is not sufficiently sustained for a composition of such length. I have had a great deal of American music sent me to look over, though when I am on the wing so constantly, there is very little time to attend to its consideration. I shall take back some of it with me, that I may go through it when I have a little leisure. A part of it interests me very much.

BROADENING ONE'S VIEWS

"Although the pianist is deeply engrossed in his work, he must not forget that there are other branches of art to be studied and loved. I find the greatest help and inspiration in studying fine paintings and in watching the trend of art in painting and sculpture. I visit art galleries and exhibitions of pictures whenever I have opportunity, or in whatever city I happen to be; for it is indeed an education for the musician to study this side of art.

"But if one thinks of sources of inspiration for the pianist, what can compare with the inspiration nature can give, in all her aspects? What can be more refreshing, after hours of hard study, than to escape to woods or fields, and enjoy nature's loveliness. And I am very fond of animals, too. After a trying rehearsal it is a complete mental diversion to visit a zoological garden and study animal life there. I did this on one occasion this season, after a hard afternoon, and found real delight in it. So much so, that I returned to the garden the next morning to have another look at the llamas. One may smile at this confession, but, to my mind, the musician should be many-sided, in order to put much into his music.

"It is difficult to secure any time for quiet work when one is engrossed in public playing. People in America have literally overwhelmed me with kindness; I cannot begin to accept all that is showered upon me. I never expected anything like it. I expected and hoped audiences would like certain things, it is true, but I was unprepared for their liking everything as they do, and with such understanding. It is indeed a great pleasure and inspiration to play for them."

XX

MME. ELLY NEY

BRING OUT THE MEANING OF THE MUSIC

WHAT a marvelous art is the Art of Piano Playing! How much of personal character, imagination, temperament, and—yes—spirituality may be expressed through those inanimate bits of ivory. A half-dozen famous pianists may play the same composition, and while all the notes will be there, while rhythm, shading, dynamics, power and delicacy are nearly matched, yet each interpretation will be quite distinct, and will not be like any of the others. Each artist will be a personality and will express himself or herself in his or her own manner.

Among the various artists who have visited America is Elly Ney, a pianist with an exceptional technic and a unique personality. The first glance at her regal figure, the imposing head with its mass of wavy brown hair, the strong, shapely hands and arms, gives the impression that here is a very powerful player, one who might, if occasion offered, tear passion to tatters. Power the pianist has in abundance, but she uses it discreetly and keeps it well in leash. She prefers to woo lovely, enticing tones from the instrument. She loves to dream before it, to weave the daintiest of tonal tracery, using as medium some of the music of the older masters. Such a medium she finds in the A minor Rondo of Mozart, which she renders with delicious clarity and grace; or the rapid flight of Mendelssohn's Rondo Capriccioso. Some of the critics have been seeking a comparison for Mme. Ney among the famous pianists of the day. One of them likens her to de Pachmann, and this comparison seems to fit her aptly so far as delicacy, clarity and fine-spun pianissimos are concerned. But her tone will be found more sympathetic, more deeply felt, more *human.*

The human side of Elly Ney is discovered when you are given the opportunity to talk to her face to face. When you know her personally you find her quite charming.

It warms the heart when she welcomes you so cordially, bids you lay aside your wraps and take the easiest chair. Then she seats herself near you, because she wants you to feel entirely at home. She apologizes for her imperfect English, but makes it, nevertheless, a medium for vivid expression. Her manner is very sincere, and

To Harriett Thomas
in remembrance
Elly Ney
Gec ... 21...

ELLY NEY

when she speaks, her whole face lights up, her
brown eyes sparkle with merriment, when they
are not regarding you with intense earnestness;
her cloud of wavy hair surrounds her face like
a halo, and her beautiful hands are most expressive.

Let us go back for a moment and glimpse the
early years of this artist. Elly Ney spent her
early childhood on the banks of the Rhine—as
she was born in Düsseldorf, of Alsatian lineage.
Her parents neither forced nor hindered her
talent, and besides her musical studies she received a thorough school education.

At the age of ten she secured a scholarship at
the Cologne Conservatory, although she was
under the age limit, but won out on the strength
of her musical gifts. At sixteen she captured the
Mendelssohn prize—a grand piano—and then
began to realize that she must become a pianist,
that this must be her life-work. Yet the road to
fame was not always easy. Her parents were
not anxious for her to follow a musical career,
and she had her early struggles to meet.

Several years were spent in Vienna, where she
at once found favor with Leschetizky and studied
with him, also with Emil Sauer. Later the young
artist traveled over Germany as pianist, and during the tour a Dutch manager heard her and

engaged her for a series of concerts in Holland, her present home country. It was in Holland that she met the Dutch violinist and conductor, Willem Van Hoogstraten, and later became his wife. It can be added that her devotion to her art has not interfered with her happy home life and companionship with her husband and their little daughter.

After this brief digression we return to the intimate talk we were just beginning with Mme. Ney.

"You heard my first recital? It was all Beethoven. For me a one-composer program is much better than one that is miscellaneous. I can throw myself into the spirit of one master more completely than into several at a time." Mme. Ney seems to feel especially *en rapport* with the music of the great master of Bonn, for it was in this university town, the birthplace of Beethoven, that she passed her early childhood.

"I am told it was a very unusual thing to begin a début recital with the *Hammerklavier* Sonata. I had some misgivings myself, before I began, as to the wisdom of the choice. But after I had played a few measures, I knew it was a good choice, for I felt the people were with me. I can always feel that. Yet such a great work as this Sonata I must play for myself alone—for I can-

not expect my audience to understand it. But I
can try to make them feel it—feel the beauty of
the music—and that is enough. I don't want
them to look at my personality; I want to put
myself out of their thought. I only want to make
the music living for them. And I must say now,
before we go farther, that American audiences
are the most appreciative in the world. It is a
great joy for me to play for them, for they understand. And if they do not always understand,
they *feel,* and they pay deep attention and follow everything, so they may learn and appreciate
better.

"It had always been a desire of mine to perform the *Hammerklavier* Sonata, but I put away
the wish, for I felt the time was not ripe—that I
was not ready. Eight years ago the temptation
came again, to begin it. But I put the thought
aside and said, 'No, I will not do it yet.' Then
at last the impulse became too strong. It was in
the summer; I had been resting and felt strong
and vigorous; I felt then I must study this most
difficult yet most soulful of all sonatas. I learned
and memorized it in three weeks."

TECHNIC PRACTISE OUTSIDE OF PIECES

In response to this question, Mme. Ney was
emphatically negative.

"No," she said, "I do not practise technic outside of pieces. I do not need to. As a child I did so, yes. In the beginning one must learn to form the hand correctly, must do scales, arpeggios, trills and exercises, must learn to put the thumb under the hand quite properly. These things once learned, however, we pass on to higher planes. As I advanced I discovered it was music itself I sought, the meaning of it, the significance of it. And in this way I train my pupils—I have taught three years in the Conservatory of Cologne. I try as soon as possible, in my teaching, to lead them from the technical side to the soulful side. Even little simple pieces have a soulful side, a theme to be brought out, a mood or picture to express. Do not misunderstand and think I make light of technical preparation. We must have it, but we can always do even this with *live* fingers, not with mechanical ones. If I put mind and feeling into my scale or trill, it is much more musical than if I play it in a purely mechanical way. We may sit and practise scales by the hour, until we become dazed by them; we can play a difficult sonata movement fifty, a hundred, five hundred times, till we become mechanical machines, and we may come no nearer the great heart of music, which is burning to be expressed."

Mr. Van Hoogstraten had entered the room and was listening attentively to our conversation.

"I used to have very pronounced ideas about the necessity for a great deal of technic practise, constantly, either on the piano, violin or any instrument, before doing much with pieces. But my wife has shown me, in her own case, and with her pupils, too, that too many hours devoted to pure technic can result in slavish bondage. It often dulls the ear and the heart to the beauty of music itself. And I believe she is right."

"Yes, it is quite true what he says; it often dulls the musical sense. For while you are giving hours and hours to scales and other technical exercises, your heart is starving."

"And another thing," continued Mr. Van Hoogstraten. "Those very scales which you do so beautifully by themselves, outside of the pieces, you never have occasion to play them just like that in pieces—in Beethoven, for instance. Your plain scales do not occur just like that in pieces, so you must learn them all over again. Is it not a waste of time—after having acquired some early facility, of course—to constantly practise scales by themselves?"

"I think it is a waste," asserted Mme. Ney. "When I go to the piano I want to make music."

And her voice was like music as she said the words.

ON MEMORIZING

"There are so many ways of memorizing. Some pianists play the piece over and over a great many times, until they know it. Others begin to learn the notes first of all, before thinking much of their meaning. I go at it differently. For me it must be the music first and the meaning of it. So I begin by thinking, thinking, thinking, studying the tones, the phrases which embody the music I wish to reproduce. I can do this away from the piano. For I don't care to hear too much the sound of the piano—not too much repetition. Better to use my mind and accomplish what I seek by mental means instead of mechanical ways.

FINGERING

"Then there is the fingering, which is so important a means of bringing out the musical idea. Certain fingers may not have heart and soul in them for the meaning to be produced; some may not have the strength. You think I do not have any weak fingers? Yes, but sometimes I have, for the strong accents required. I learned the

Hammerklavier Sonata with a particular fingering, and found later that I should use other fingers in places, to bring out certain effects. So that part of the work had to be done over. The pianist must choose the use of fingers to suit her hand, and her understanding of the music.

BEFORE AN AUDIENCE

"Do I always play the piece the same way? Oh, never!" and the pianist shook her curls emphatically. "How can one play a piece even before an audience always the same way? One is not a machine. In every public appearance the surroundings are different, one's mood is never just the same, and, last but not least, the audience is always different. I feel at once the mental touch of the listeners, whether it is sympathetic or not; we react on each other. I feel all this, even though I seem to be—and am—completely absorbed in what I am playing. An audience can be—often is—the artist's inspiration. I am never quite sure just how I shall play a piece until I have tried it on an audience. Then I really find the inner meaning by the way the piece impresses the audience, and the response I receive from the sympathetic listener. Then I really begin to study the work in the highest way. In the light of this thought it can easily be seen that I must be constantly remodeling and polishing, here a little more tone, there a bit less; here a pause, there more of a ritard. The art of the interpreter is constant recreation. The audience is the greatest teacher of all.

VELOCITY

"It seems to me that too often the great aim in piano playing appears to be rapidity, when the aim should really be to *make music*. Rapidity often takes away all the feeling, the meaning of the music. Of course, one must be able to play with quickness, but not at the sacrifice of clearness and understanding. These must stand first. And then the character of the music must be considered. If a beautiful theme of Beethoven or Mozart is played too fast, as is often the case, it is spoiled for those who understand. And why? Why should it be done? Is it to show that the pianist has fleet fingers? The truth is that it is far more difficult to play more slowly and preserve a beautiful rhythm and the dignity of the composer's meaning, than to rush through at greater speed. Ah, if such players would only realize this great fact.

ARTISTIC CONSCIENCE

"One must preserve and reproduce the meaning of the music before anything else. One must play cleanly, to make this meaning clear. If at any time I miss a note, or even a small phrase does not come out as I wish, it makes me very unhappy. I go at once to the unfortunate spot and fix the passage more firmly in mind. And with my pupils it is the same; no note is allowed to be played carelessly, or not in a clean way. And if pupils play in public and make a slip or play wrong notes, I am as unhappy as though I had done it myself. One must be so careful of every point, both in playing and teaching."

We might have talked on for hours, so full was Mme. Ney of the subject of sympathetic music study, but time, for her, was pressing. Her principal theme, to which she constantly reverted, was to "make music" out of every good composition. And good music was alone worthy of consideration. To place the expressive and soulful above the merely mechanical, the spiritual above the material, in her art, is the earnest aim of this pianist. In a time when marvelous technical feats are so highly lauded, we need to be reminded, sometimes, of the great fact that these things, although they are necessary to a degree, are not the end and aim of great piano playing. It should rather be the sincere desire of every artist of the keyboard, worthy the name, to reveal the high, noble and spiritual side, without which there can be no great interpretation.

XXI

ALEXANDRE BOROWSKI

A NATURAL TECHNIC

WHEN Alexandre Borowski stepped upon the platform of Carnegie Hall, New York, to give his first early season recital in America, he was practically unknown to the great audience that greeted him. He had come to this country very quietly—indeed, almost unheralded—and the musicians and music lovers in the audience, who had merely heard his name, could not help wondering what he would be like and how he would play. We imagined he must be considered one of the great ones, or he would not choose our largest auditorium for his début; but we would soon know.

After the first half-hour, we felt pretty sure Borowski belonged to the inner circle. Here was a piano tone, rich and warm in quality; here was great power mated with gossamer lightness and delicacy. And here was an astonishing technic, that could work up brilliant climaxes, both intense and thrilling. The big organ Toccata of Bach, transcribed by Busoni, was massive and architectural, while a characteristic Larghetto of Mozart, which followed, was delightful in its sweet simplicity. And so throughout the evening the new artist conquered everything he attempted, including the audience.

"I only intend giving two concerts here this year," said the artist, when he had the opportunity to confer on musical subjects, "though I shall probably return to you next season. I come to you now from Russia, by way of South America. That is a great country—South America—and a country of music lovers. I played many concerts there, but felt it would be wiser for me to limit my New York appearances to two concerts. This will give me a little leisure to look about your wonderful city and get used to the, to me, new piano. In Europe most artists play the Bechstein, a very beautiful instrument. What the Bechstein is over there the Steinway is in America. But I was unfamiliar with it when I came, and this made my first concert difficult for me. I shall have time before my second recital to become thoroughly used to the new instrument.

"Yes, I began to play the piano at a very early age, but never was a *wunderkind*. It seems to me that talented children, who are exploited in public in early years, often become blasé later on, and lose their ambition to carry their art to the highest development. I know I should have felt so. But I was not forced along the artistic path. I was just a normal, healthy boy, taking music together with school work.

EARLY STUDIES

"My first piano teacher was my mother, who had been a pupil of Safonoff. I began to study when I was seven years old. Later I went to the Conservatory and had Mme. Annette Essipoff for a teacher. This was in Petrograd. Along with music, which at that time was not the most important subject which occupied my days, I applied myself with ardor to other studies, especially to jurisprudence, with the result that I completed the course with honors and was graduated a full-fledged lawyer. I could now practise law, if I so desired.

"But as I had made satisfactory progress in music during this whole period, it was considered I had talent for that, and the inclination for it as well. It was urged upon me to give up law and devote myself to art. After careful thought, and following the wishes of my family and friends, I relinquished the idea of becoming a jurist and gave my whole time, thought, and energy to perfecting myself in musical art.

"I finished my musical course in 1912, and was thereafter free to begin my career. I started at once to give concerts, and played in many parts of my own country. Three years later found me in Moscow, at the head of a Master Class of young artist students. My contract permitted me, while holding these classes, to fulfill as many concert dates as I wished. So I made various concert tours over Europe, whenever possible. This Master Class I speak of was made up of thoroughly trained players, really concert pianists, who were familiar with most of the literature of the piano.

"These young players were divided into several classes. The members of each class met once a week. As I had five or six of these classes, I was occupied at least every other day. There were ten or twelve players in a class, and they studied the most difficult works in piano repertoire. They brought a piece but once to class, for after it had been criticized they were supposed to finish, polish and master it by themselves. So you see they must have been advanced students to be able to do this.

NATURAL TECHNIC

"How did I acquire my technic? I hardly know. No doubt some of it is natural. I can state this: that I have never practised technic for itself alone, never pure technic—so called—outside of pieces, never scales, chords, trills or octaves, except as they have come in pieces. As I have already studied so much of the literature of the piano, I have myself discovered most of the technical problems in piano playing from the compositions I have been through. I can also say that I have never found it necessary to devote so much of the day to practise as many pianists think they must do. I never practise more than two and a half or three hours a day; that amount is quite sufficient.

ON MEMORIZING

"I am told I have an unusual memory. Perhaps this may be true, for I feel my ability to memorize is somewhat out of the ordinary. Of course you know Balakireff's *Islamey*. It has been called, you remember, about the most difficult piano piece ever written. I both learned and committed it to memory in five days. How did I do it? It is visual memory with me. I see the notes and signs on the printed page before me as

I play. No, I do not seem to hear them so much as see them.

"No, I do not care for modern music in general—as the term is at present understood. Of course, there are a few exceptions, as there are bound to be. I put the Sonata by the Frenchman Auric, and also my arrangement of the Carnival, from Stravinsky's *Petroushka,* on a New York program, so you see I play twentieth century music. I like to combine eighteenth and twentieth century works. Thus I am much interested in the old music of Bach, Handel, Rameau and Scarlatti. What meat is there in grand old Bach's music! Those Suites of his—especially the English Suites—how delightful they are—but so difficult. Here is the Sixth, on which I am now at work," and turning to the piano (we were sitting in my studio at the time), he played parts of the Suite in question, especially rapid portions, which he reaffirmed were "so difficult."

"You see," he continued, "this music must be played without a flaw, and that is why one must study it so carefully and accurately. No, I do not necessarily mean each hand alone, but rather taking out the specially difficult passages, which must be gone over many hundreds of times, before they reach perfection.

"As I said a moment ago, I am more in sympathy with music of the classic and present time, rather than the music of the nineteenth century, or romantic period. I play little Chopin in public, as it is music not so congenial to me. And then I feel the player must be especially gifted in certain ways to play Chopin well. He must be capable of entering into the meaning of all the forms and movements of this composer's music, or he cannot be called a thoroughly equipped Chopin player. For instance, he may play the Nocturnes and Valses, the Preludes and Études —yes, even the Sonatas—and yet not be able to enter into the subtle rhythm and meaning of the Mazurkas. Of all Chopin's works, I consider the Mazurkas the most difficult—those and the Ballades. Thus, unless the pianist has the temperament and understanding to enter into these, he cannot be called a comprehensive Chopin interpreter, in all that word implies.

"Yes, I have a very large repertoire and am constantly adding to it. While I was in South America I gave many concerts in various cities. In Buenos Aires I gave twelve entirely different programs in ten weeks. I play much Russian music, of course—Scriabine, Prokofieff and many others. But I play the music of all countries and all epochs. American music and MacDowell?

Very little American music is known in Russia, I think. As for MacDowell, of course we know him by name, and a few of the more brilliant numbers, such as the *Hexen Tanz,* Polonaise and Concerto for piano, but not the Sonatas. I should like to do one or more of these, and also some works by other American composers. Now that I have been in America, the musical growth of your country interests me immensely. I have had a happy two months here, and I hope to return for a longer stay. But now, after our two happy months, Madame and I are on the point of returning to Europe, as I have a tour of forty concerts on the other side, which will take me to London, Paris, Spain, Italy, Belgium, Holland and Germany. But all the time I shall look forward to my return to your beautiful country —America!"

XXII

SERGE PROKOFIEFF

FUTURISM IN MUSIC

A FEW facts about that remarkable pianist and composer, Serge Prokofieff, have been furnished by V. G. Karatygin, Professor of Musical History, in Leningrad. The Professor, glimpsing the achievements of his subject from early years, said in part:

Serge Prokofieff was born in the estate of Sontsovka, South Russia, April 11, 1891. He showed evidence of natural musical ability at the very earliest age—a "leitmotiv" of all famous musicians. His mother was his first teacher, who later passed him on to Professors Janeieff and Glière. His first manuscripts belong to the age of six!

In 1904 young Serge, then only thirteen, entered the St. Petersburg Conservatory, from which he was graduated with highest honors, winning the coveted Rubinstein prize. Here he studied composition under Rimsky-Korsakoff and Liadoff, piano with the famous pianist, An-

nette Essipoff, and conducting with Tscherepnine. Due to the technical possibilities in the construction of his hands, with their long, tenacious
fingers, Prokofieff soon became a remarkable pianist. His ease in managing the piano induced
him to first compose for that instrument. He also
tried his hand at opera at the tender age of seven,
and again at nine. At the age of eleven he composed a Symphony in four parts, at twelve a
third opera. As he grew older his imagination
worked even more energetically. During the
first years at the Conservatory he wrote over
one hundred works, a fourth opera, *Undina,*
another Symphony in three parts, six piano
Sonatas, and over ninety other piano pieces. One
of these early Sonatas was revised and published
in 1909 as Opus 1. In 1911 the First Concerto
for piano appeared, and in 1912 the Second
Sonata. The next year the Second Concerto saw
the light; in 1917 came the Third and Fourth
Sonatas.

There is no musician who does not know the
originality of Prokofieff's music—daring, tur-
bulent and full of life and power as it is. It is
true many musicians cannot accept this music
because it frequently, in impassioned moments,
oversteps the rules of harmony and counterpoint.
But Prokofieff, while violating academic laws,

is always logical. His music is marked by genuine truth and sometimes you will discover moments of revelation. He does not care to follow well-beaten paths, but prefers to force his way through virgin forests, putting aside all obstacles with masterful hand, breaking trees and jumping over broad streams. Much noise and rumbling accompany him in his wandering toward new shores. His daring has always a strong and convincing logic. The course of his ship is straight and determined, and leads toward the sun, toward the fulness of life and joy of existence.

In listening to this music we feel its invincible strength, enormous temperament, rich thematic imagination, remarkable harmonic inventiveness. It is painting with broad strokes—even touching the grotesque. There is astonishing boldness and energy in it, alternating with flashes of humor. It is quite wonderful music! You are bitten, pinched, burnt, but you do not revolt. He has some kinship with the American, Edgar Allan Poe. But here and there you will be touched by something tender, gentle, sweet. There are occasional pearls of fine musical poetry, especially precious when contrasted by some of the boiling, rushing music. This lyrical current is to be felt in the Sonatas. The lyrical theme of the Third

Sonata is one of the composer's most fortunate achievements.

Besides the Sonatas, Prokofieff has written many shorter pieces for the piano. There are some twenty *Moments Fugitifs,* a set of Études, some *Miniatures,* some Preludes, a Scherzo, a charming Gavotte, five *Sarcasms,* and more than a score of vivid tone pictures and Dances.

Knowing all this before the arrival of the brilliant Russian, for his first concert tour in America, his first appearance as pianist was an event of musical importance.

PROKOFIEFF THE PIANIST

The large audience sat waiting expectantly—waiting for what? A new light from Russia, it was said. One was inclined to ask: Can anything great come out of Russia *now?* From out all that chaos and red-handed turmoil, shall we get sweet harmonies, pleasant thoughts and sounds? Or will the music of Russia reflect the present conditions of the country? We shall soon know.

Meanwhile the house filled with the cream of Metropolitan musical life. Composers were there, and conductors, pianists and singers. There were many others who did not belong to these divisions, but looked as though they had

come out of Russia, Japan or some other country
on the oposite side of the globe. One saw many
nationalities represented; also many of our teachers were in its makeup as well. It was indeed a
cosmopolitan audience—all waiting for a new
sensation.

What will he look like, this new light, and how
will he play? Like a composer or a virtuoso?
Will his music have the flavor, the qualities, of the
Russian music with which we are already familiar? Will it be anything like the music of
Rachmaninoff, who is in the audience today?
For we have grown somewhat accustomed to his
idiom by now. Or will it be strange, weird,
cacophonous? We shall know what it will be
like in a few moments.

Ah, the stage door opens—the door which
separates the newcomer from the New World to
which he is to lay siege. If that small door could
only speak, what could it not reveal of shivering
suspense and shaking nerves—of brave determination to do, or—

A young man steps out briskly from the door-
way and marches to the instrument. He evidently believes in the old axiom, which may apply
to the concert platform as well as to any other
spot or situation in life: that time and tide—the
audience—wait for no man.

He seats himself as quickly as he came, and plunges at once into work, without hesitation or delay. Four Études of his own follow each other in quick succession; then a big Sonata, in four movements. The instant the last note is struck, the pianist-composer rises abruptly and retires as briskly as he has come.

As soon as the audience could recover breath, it began to consider what had been happening, what had been heard. A buzz of voices could be heard all over the hall; the critics gathered in small groups, shaking their wise heads and consulting in undertones. No one could deny that here was a composer of torrential temperament, who feared not to assail the ears of the listeners with the most complex dissonances, if he cannot secure the effects he seeks in any pleasanter way. Power of tone he has in abundance, also marvelous velocity. But it is also true that quality of tone is often more potent to conquer and enslave the hearer. He has scarcely arrived at the point where he believes that after the whirlwind may come "the still small voice." Doubtless one day the fiery young artist may discover the potency of this small voice, and then his playing will take on a delicacy and tenderness not at present discoverable. For now he is all fire and flame, though at rare moments, when he did play softly, he secured an excellent singing tone; we longed for more of those moments.

But his playing and his music made an undeniable appeal, through its very daring and bizarre strangeness. It was like tasting a new kind of spice which bit the tongue. The tang was pungent, but not altogether unpleasant; one was not averse to tasting again, and then again. At least the audience seemed to think so, for it remained to applaud and call for encores after the long all-Russian program was finished.

The critics departed to write wisely, about "biceps," "triceps," "wrists of steel" and other things they thought they discovered in the new pianist. The conservatives decided his music was all dreadful cacophony, and they resented having their eardrums assailed so mercilessly. Those with ears open to new ideas, new effects, new surprises and sensations, rather liked it all and were quite willing to listen further—were open to conviction. They had faith to believe that future hearings would reveal new excellences and beauties hidden on first acquaintance. For had it not been said by an authority in his own country:

"It is from Serge Prokofieff that we can expect new ideas in musical art, more and more deep and individual."

Taking this to heart, we resolve to endeavor to

understand this strange music and its remarkable interpreter.

THE PIANIST-COMPOSER AT HOME

Serge Prokofieff has a studio in a hotel in the heart of the metropolis. Here are his piano, his music and manuscripts—his tools.

He entered this workroom to greet the visitor, one afternoon, with the same *presto* movements that he makes when he walks out on the stage to play a recital. He is quick-spoken, too, with a surprising facility in English, considering the short time he has had at his disposal to become familiar with it. "I speak six languages— French, Italian, Spanish, German, Russian and some English," he asserted calmly, with his pleasant, broad smile, as though to know six tongues were the easiest thing in the world.

"How did you acquire your wonderful piano technic?" he was asked.

"What is?"

"Your piano technic—how did you get it?"

"Oh, yes, I will tell you. There are some pianists who must practise many hours every day; again there are some others who do not work very much—technic to them seems to be a gift of the gods. I think I must belong to the latter class, for I do not need so much to practise; my hands do not forget," and he held up a wonderful hand, with long, supple fingers.

Then the fiery young Russian took a few turns up and down the room, just to work off superfluous energy, before settling down again in his chair.

"You see," he continued, "it took me some time to reach here after I left my home in Russia; it was a long, roundabout journey. So, for over five months I was without a piano at all. Then, after arriving in America, I had only a short time to prepare the program for my first recital; maybe but two weeks to learn those Rachmaninoff Preludes—three of them. I was very anxious about them, and a bit nervous, when I knew the composer himself was in the audience at my début.

"Yes, I have read many of the criticisms. Some of them say my music is cerebral; that is said in Russia, too. But about 'biceps' and 'triceps,' I do not quite understand. What is? Can you explain those words, applied to piano playing?"

CRITICISM AN ART IN RUSSIA

Without waiting for a specific reply, he went on:

"When a critic in my country has to write about the music of a new composer, or a new

pianist, he considers it a really serious matter.
He makes it his business to learn all he can about
that pianist or that music, in the first place.
Then he calls upon the musician, asks him to describe the pieces and play them for him. He will
hear them three—four—five times; so he has a
very good idea of their form and meaning, also
the playing of the pianist, before attempting to
say anything about them in print. All this is
not too much trouble for the conscientious critic,
for he wishes to give the artist the best possible
review in his power. But such does not seem to
be the method of the critics in your country."

He broke off and looked searchingly at the
visitor.

"About composing. I hardly know when I
began to compose. When I was seven I wrote
an opera, for a little family fête-day. It had no
orchestra, only a piano accompaniment. The
words were by our greatest poet, Pushkin. We
all had much pleasure out of this little story set
to music. My next effort in this direction happened two years later, when I wrote another
opera, a little bit more elaborate, but still without
orchestra.

"When I was eleven, I composed a symphony
in four parts, and at twelve a third opera, which
this time had an orchestral background. For by

this time I had begun to study theory and composition. I made those studies with Gliére, Rimsky-Korsakoff and Liadoff. When I was thirteen, I entered the Petrograd Conservatory, and from then on my whole time was given to musical and other studies. I really studied seriously. Mme. Annette Essipowa was my teacher in piano there. You, of course, know her in your country, as she once toured America.

"From the formation of my hand and fingers, I always found it very easy to play piano. And as it was so easy to play piano, I wrote quite a good deal of piano music. I have already four piano Sonatas, and a number of groups of short pieces. You heard my Second Sonata; I shall play the others later. I am always working, always composing—thinking out new effects, new forms of expression. They say my music is material rather than spiritual; perhaps they mean it is subjective; I seem to embody in music real people, real scenes and episodes."

The above is a brief glimpse of the personality and work of the Prokofieff who came to America five years ago. Later he came to direct his fantastic opera, *The Love of the Three Oranges,* which was given by the Chicago Opera Company and was also seen in New York.

Serge Prokofieff, the Rubinstein prize-winner,

the militant virtuoso, composer and performer, is one of the remarkable figures in contemporary Russian music. To repeat the words of Professor Katarygin:

"It is from Serge Prokofieff, more than any one else, that Russia will look for new ideas in musical art—more and more deep and individual."

XXIII

GEORGE LIEBLING

DETERMINATION TO SUCCEED CONQUERS

To meet and talk with George Liebling brings back memories of student days in Berlin, when all the world was young, and every event a wonderful experience. Mr. Liebling was, in those days, a rising young pianist and a professor in the Kullak Conservatorium.

A few days before the first concert of his second American season, we were chatting in the drawing-room of his hotel, with Mme. Liebling not far away, and the artist was recalling some of the events and experiences of earlier years. We will let him recount them in his own delightfully vivid manner.

"My earlier studies in piano were made with Theodore Kullak, head of the well-known conservatory which bears his name. I had been thoroughly grounded by him in the technical side of my art, for he was a very careful teacher, and I had studied industriously to master its literature.

"When Theodore Kullak passed away and his son, Franz Kullak, was in command, I was uncertain just what to do. I felt I should have more guidance; I was not quite ready to strike out for myself, being very young at the time. In those days my means were small, but at least my hair was long, and I felt I was destined to become an artist. I stated my case to Kullak, and concluded by saying, 'Master, what do you advise?'

" 'If you desire to work with me for a while—that is, if you think I can help you—you can do so for one year. The other difficulty you mention can be overcome, for I will make you a professor in the Conservatory,' which he did. Somewhat later he said to me: 'I know you desire to study with Liszt. He is getting on in years, as he is now eighty-two. I would advise your going to him at once, for if you should miss this opportunity you would always regret it.'

"I acted on his suggestion, and to the famous Master Liszt I went forthwith.

"Yes, Liszt was a great teacher as well as a marvelous artist. At that time I consider there were only two real teachers in the world—Liszt and Leschetizky. They were each unique, individual, and very different one from the other. Each one had labored prodigiously to perfect his

George Liebling

mechanism and to evolve a super-technic which should be absolutely complete, unassailable, flawless. This is only saying that a truly great artist must conquer every technical difficulty, because only through such unhampered means can he truly express his highest self, his highest ideals in his art. Art begins where technic ends. All the same, we must have this technical background before we can begin to express our true feeling in playing. When we have this sense of technical mastery, then we feel free and can express ourselves spontaneously. Theodore Kullak once said: 'Why talk of expression until the fingers are capable of expression.' "

Mr. Liebling speaks English with great fluency (as he also does a number of other languages), for he lived eight years in London. He smiles slyly when he relates that Americans, unfamiliar with this fact, marvel at his mastery of their language. "America is a wonderful country," he said; "we have already taken out our first papers and shall become citizens in about four years' time. But this is a little digression.

"You ask how the master, Liszt, taught us. Liszt's classes met twice a week and lasted about two hours. From forty to fifty persons might be present, but of those perhaps only ten or a dozen might be asked to play. These, the real players, were favorites of the master; the others, who sat around the sides of the room, seldom or never had the opportunity to take part. Among the little group of concert pianists were such names as d'Albert, Sauer, Siloti, Lamond, Friedheim, Reisenauer, and the rest. I was the youngest of them all.

"On entering the salon, we all put our music on the piano. When Liszt entered, he would go and see what selections had been offered. He would take up one and ask, 'Who brings this piece to us today?' If the answer came from one who was a rather mediocre player, he would lay it down again with the remark: 'Oh, I've heard that piece so often lately; we won't have it today —some other time will do.' Looking further, he would take up another with the same question. If this belonged to one of the favored group, and especially if it happened to be one of his own compositions, he would say: 'Ah, yes, I haven't heard this in a very long time; we will have it today.' If the compositions chosen were concertos or lengthy works, not more than four or five could be gone over at a single meeting, so that only a few of us had a chance to play each time.

"The master never descended to speak of the technical side of piano playing; it was the interpretation of the piece, always, that was discussed. And he could illumine the passage in question with a word or two, or even with a glance or movement. Yes, he was wonderful as a teacher. I was with him two years and learned a very great deal.

"Then came the time when I must start on my career, and I toured Germany and Austria, played in Russia and other places.

"One day it came to me very strongly that my technical equipment was not entirely impeccable; I had not gained absolute mastery over my instrument and myself. I determined to stop concertizing at once, and seclude myself to work on my technic till I had conquered it completely. I was in Russia then, and stayed in a little, quiet, out-of-the-way hotel where no one knew me, went nowhere and just worked. I give you my word, I practised ten and eleven hours a day. That was real work. After one year's time I emerged from my retreat and returned to Germany. My playing had so changed that my friends did not even recognize it, and compared it with Rosenthal or de Pachmann. I often think it would be a good plan for artists to play behind a curtain. Then the audience would just listen to music and not be influenced by personality.

"Yes, I have taught almost countless pupils,

though naturally only those more or less advanced. I have had my own schools in Berlin, London and Dresden, and can say I have been successful with them all. I have never had a pupil leave me; I have sometimes left a pupil.

"When a new pupil comes, I put certain questions to test her mentality, her tastes and inclinations. I am a doctor, who must know how to prescribe for every ailment; or, like a gardener, I must know the proper soil and treatment for each plant, so as to cultivate the finest blossoms. I require—as every earnest teacher must—that the student have absolute confidence in what I tell her. And I expect entire obedience. Even if I tell her to practise but ten minutes a day, she must obey as readily as though I asked for ten hours. The student must be loyal; if unwilling to be, she must seek another master.

"What material do I use?" The artist gave me one of his quizzical little smiles. "I use everything—whatever is needful. Of course, I expect good hand position, with firm fingers. But this subject varies with the individual. Kullak taught a somewhat arched position; Leschetizky favored a higher arch and a lower wrist. I use a great deal of Czerny. Yes, Op. 740, of course. I have just had published a special edition of the seventh Étude, Book 1, of 740. If you remember, this is built on little figures containing repeated notes. There are four sixteenths to a beat. I have increased the number to six, which renders the Étude more useful as a study and more brilliant as a bravura piece. I play it in concert.

"The technical material I use for my own practise? Ah, well, every artist must have his own routine of technical forms—the things he has found most useful, most indispensable for his mechanical well-being. These no artist will reveal; these are my secret.

"One of my secrets, however, I will give you. It is this. The player who would become an artist, who would succeed in his chosen calling, must have the will to conquer. He must be determined to win. Nothing must stand in the way; no lack of energy or determination must hold him back. I believe that, given a certain amount of ability, one can make of himself what he will. He can be a master, if he determines to be. He can conquer if he will pay the price. And the price is only a pleasure and satisfaction to one who loves his art.

"Some artists who are pianistically well equipped for public life, find it too exhaustive, or are too nervous of temperament to endure the strain. Anton Rubinstein, they say, suffered tortures before facing an audience. I seem to be differently constituted. I am never so happy as when I am on the platform, playing. I am like a high-mettled horse who is eager for the race. My fingers tingle for contact with the keys; my ears tingle in anticipation of the tones I shall produce. I thoroughly enjoy my task, and, as I said, I am never happier than in thus exercising my art for others.

"In the program I shall give in New York is a Concerto of my own, quite a serious work, in which my nephew and former pupil, Leonard Liebling, will accompany me. There will also be a group of three original short pieces. One, a valse, is very taking and catchy, and is not at all difficult. A pupil who has studied only two or three years can do it."

XXIV

MARIA CARRERAS

FINDING TECHNICAL MATERIAL IN PIECES

"I FEEL as though I knew you very well indeed, although we have never spoken together," was Mme. Carreras' greeting when I called at her beautiful home overlooking the Hudson, one August afternoon. "How do I know you so well? From your writings—your intimate glimpses of keyboard artists. Such intimate, personal glimpses seem to me much more interesting than a mere interview without them."

She led the way into her music-room, which contained not only the grand piano and masses of music—an artist's tools—but many artistic souvenirs from the countries where she had traveled and played, as well as portraits and mementos of the great in music and art.

To meet Mme. Carreras is to come in touch with a truly artistic nature, keenly responsive to various forms of art expression.

"It is unfortunate," she says, "when the pianist is a person of one idea, wedded to one form of art; when it can be said of him, that he 'cares for nothing but music,' or that he 'knows nothing but music.' I feel strongly that the musician, or more particularly the pianist, needs to broaden his outlook on art and life through a study of other art forms besides his own. The world about him is teeming with wonderful things. Let him study the wonders of nature, and strive to reproduce his impressions, not only in his playing, but on canvas, if he will, or in words of poetry or prose. Or, if he have no creative ability outside of music, he can at least learn from what others have done. He can read and study the masterpieces of literature, he can visit the galleries and feast his eyes and his soul on the treasures of painting and sculpture to be found there. Is this not better for his own development than to sit toiling at his instrument eight or nine hours a day? And for what? To become a mechanical machine? For that is the result of closing his eyes and shutting his soul from the wonderful opportunities that can be had for the asking, if he will just reach out and take them. He owes it to himself and his art to be awake to all artistic influences.

"How true it is that the mentality of the pianist determines what he will make of himself. He can be either narrow and pedantic or broad-minded and receptive in his art expression. One person will be shut up to his own little daily round of routine, while another, though faithful to his studies, will open his mind and heart to kindred forms of art, that lie within his reach. Is it not so?" and Madame raised her dark eyes with a brilliant smile.

"As you see, I am not in favor of excessive practise at the piano; it's almost a crime to spend seven or eight hours at the instrument each day. Four hours should be ample. But—and this is imperative—those hours must be spent in complete concentration with the work in hand. No half-way study will bring results. The mind must know what the fingers should do and are doing.

"Do I practise technic for itself alone? No, I do not, and I cannot recall that I ever did. I began to play piano when I was five, and one hardly remembers what one did at five. It seems to me I have always played the instrument, as I can scarcely remember the time when I did not play.

"I studied with Sgambati in Rome and made my début in that city when I was fifteen. Perhaps the greatest influence in my life, however, was Busoni. Ah, there was a truly great musician! He is my ideal of a many-sided artist. He was not only a pianist but a composer, and beyond that he was a painter. His mind was open to many forms of art. He was also an accomplished linguist, speaking a number of languages besides his own.

"With all this depth of knowledge, he cared nothing for display, and never played to the gallery. He was entirely devoid of commercialism, and would never lower his art for financial gain. I do not think he was understood in America, either as artist or man, and he was conscious of this fact. Perhaps this threw him back upon himself, and he became more reserved and inaccessible to Americans than he would otherwise have been.

"About the time Busoni took up his residence in Bologna, as Director of the Liceo, and Conductor of the Symphony Orchestra—in 1913—I met and played for him. When I finished, he said:

" 'No, you do not need lessons from me, but you need me as a friend—you need my friendship.'

"This was, of course, a great happiness for me. From that time on I saw him very often, several times a week. We played together, we discussed this and that great work for its meaning and interpretation; we talked of many forms of art. His broad learning was of the greatest help, and became a source of true inspiration to me. As I have already said, I have learned more from this master mind than from any other person or source.

IN PIANO TEACHING

"Naturally the students who seek my help are not beginners. I never take those. With older students I do not insist on scales and other technical exercises outside of pieces. There is so much material in the pieces themselves, which can be used to advantage, if the pupil is shown how to use it. Pieces must be thoroughly analyzed, and all difficult passages worked out in special technical forms, in order to get the utmost benefit from this kind of study.

"In the matter of finger action, I do not advise excessive high action. Some players hold the knuckles low, and then find they must raise their fingers with an effort in order to get them high enough to ensure clearness of touch. This will not be necessary if the hand assumes a higher arch. In that case the fingers have more freedom, since they play from a greater height, and therefore do not need to be lifted so high."

Mme. Carreras illustrated this point by placing her hand in the desired position on a table near her. One could not help admire this perfectly formed and developed piano hand as she posed it convincingly.

"This was also Busoni's idea—to arch the hand and hold knuckles high, which rendered excessively high finger action unnecessary.

"In adjusting hands to the keyboard, when playing, I would avoid twisting them about, or jerking them in and out among the black keys, or putting them out of normal position in any unnecessary way. A little forethought and calculation of movement will obviate this difficulty, and the player will gain in smoothness and velocity. Another example of adjustment is seen when an ascending scale in double thirds is played in right hand. In order that the passage shall flow smoothly, with no jerks or twists, the hand is turned *outward,* with wrist held *inward,* like this——" The pianist seated herself at the piano and played the passage with smoothness and swiftness, while the hand and arm remained in the position indicated.

"I have just returned from Cincinnati, where I have taught a large class of young players. What did I find they needed most? The study of sounds—or perhaps you would say tones— and their various qualities. This, of course, is a great study, and one that young students have

not thought so much about. It is a very necessary
study in order to render the playing expressive
and varied in tone quality. The pedal, naturally,
is a wonderful aid in this search for tone quality,
but is a subject much neglected among students
generally. They find they have a great deal
to learn along this line.

"Another subject which the majority of students do not sufficiently consider is the phrasing.
Not to understand the phrase comes from lack
of analysis of the composition. An understanding of phrasing should indeed be clearly grasped,
if the playing is to be intelligent and convey the
meaning of the composition to those who listen.
The player must have a clear mental grasp of
these things before she can convey them through
her performance.

"A subject of the greatest importance is the
pause in playing, yet few students seem to realize its value. If allowed to do it, they would
hurry through a piece without a break anywhere,
satisfied if they reproduce the notes. But a
musical composition must have pauses of shorter
or longer duration, just as language is punctu-
ated with the comma, semicolon and period. All
this requires much thought and proves how
wholly mental is the work of the pianist.

"In my classes this summer I played much for

the students, illustrating every point as it came up. We analyzed each piece; I required the player to dissect it for keys, chords, modulation, structure and meaning. Difficult passages were practised in various rhythms, and technical exercises formed from them. I enjoyed my work there, and I think the students made commendable progress. I shall probably return there next summer. In the winter I have little or no time for teaching, though I give a lesson here and there between concert engagements.

MODERN MUSIC

"I do not care very much for modern music. There are occasionally a few compositions which are quite nice, but so many others are unpleasant or positively ugly. My favorite composers are Bach, Beethoven, Chopin, Liszt. Of course I play much Schumann, too, and many old masters as well as such new ones as are nice. But the four I mention surely contain food for the mind and heart of any pianist."

Apropos of Mme. Carreras' playing of Liszt, one noted American critic remarked: "The pianist gave another evidence of her capacity in Liszt's *Petrarca Sonnette,* not the facsimile of a ruthless virtuoso, but an impression of a poet communing with a poet."

Of her own career as pianist, Mme. Carreras speaks thus:

"I have played in about every country on the globe, and have a record of over nineteen hundred concerts. In South America I played in some of the largest cities, giving sixteen concerts in six weeks in Sao Paolo, the home town of Guiomar Novaes. I also played in Buenos Aires and other cities in that part of the country. I have only been in North America between two and three years, and have already played eight times in New York."

The Italian pianist did not give these facts in any boastful spirit, but simply in answer to the visitor's inquiry. By nature she is very genial and sincere, and as an artist is one of the distinguished masters of the keyboard.

XXV

BERYL RUBINSTEIN

THE PIANIST AS TEACHER

WHEN does the artist really come into his own —artistically speaking? He has labored from infancy, perhaps, to master a chosen instrument. Into this labor has gone a daily routine of technical study. Touch had to be rendered sure and dependable; tone developed in every possible degree of quality and color. Velocity, delicacy, power, brilliancy, all had to be acquired by hours, days—years of tireless effort. And even then all this is only the background—these are merely the materials of his art. The facility gained in their use must be applied to repertoire, which must be built up piece by piece—one at a time— stones in the art-edifice he is erecting. Each stone must be cut and polished to its highest capacity by talent, hard work and experience.

Then on a higher plane—on the spiritual side —so much must go into the development and perfecting of each composition and its interpretation. All this takes years of constant, unremitting effort, of devotion to an ideal. When at last the hour comes for the fulfillment of this lifelong struggle, when the worker can realize his dream, and awakes to know he is an artist—awakes to realize he can express himself through the composer's thought and can make the listener feel with him—then he can rejoice, for he now knows it is possible to accomplish what he will.

Thoughts like these came to mind in listening to a recent recital by Beryl Rubinstein. American audiences have watched the artistic growth of this pianist from a gifted child to his present high attainments. Here are all the excellencies of the mature artist—smooth, effortless technic, delicacy, power, velocity. Beyond and above these is now the power and ability to project the meaning of the music with convincing force. On the program just heard was placed the Liszt B minor Sonata, a work to test the technical and interpretative ability of any player. Rubinstein surmounted every obstacle and set the noble work before us with a virility, a tenderness, an exaltation I have never heard surpassed. This is high praise, but I have heard all great pianists play it, and feel I can speak from experience.

In conferring later with the young artist in regard to piano technic, teaching and playing, we took up the following points, one after another, as he is doing much teaching as well as playing.

The question of hand position came up first.

" 'Do I teach arched hand position and distinct finger action in early stages?' you ask. It seems to me there can be no decided rule for anything so individual as position, or even as piano technic. No two pianists play exactly alike. One's technic is just as much a part of one as one's interpretations are. We hear much of the Leschetizky method, or system, or whatever name you choose to give it. Compare the technic or pianistic mechanism of these four distinguished products of the Leschetizky school: Paderewski, Gabrilowitsch, Friedman and Zeisler. The mechanism of each one of these is different from all the others.

"Personally, I think an arched hand—that is, with the knuckles forming the top of the arch— means a strong hand. And a strong hand, pianistically speaking, means the instrument of a well-developed technic. There are pianists who do not play with arched hand, yet possess a splendid technical equipment.

"As to distinct finger action in the early stages —I think that distinct finger action, with fingers lifted reasonably high, is an excellent idea. For such strenuous movement of the fingers acts as a means of developing strength. Gradually this high movement can be toned down to suit one's ideas of tone production. I have a very talented little pupil whom I have been teaching for the past five years. During the first three years he was with me I quite wore myself out trying to make him lift his fingers and not play with them flat on the keys. But at last I found my efforts were quite useless and finally perceived that, in his case, they were not necessary. This boy, at the age of fourteen, has a mature technic, as honest and legitimate as that of any player of twice his years. And it is a well rounded development. There are few things beyond him, technically. He will certainly be heard of one of these days. His name is Lionel Novak.

" 'The study of octaves and what material to use in teaching them?'

"Octaves should be relaxed, in arm and wrist (as everything else), whether they are played from the wrist, the forearm, the upper arm, or by the combined use of all three. I hate to see people play octaves or chords as though they were afraid of them. Kullak Octave Studies serve as well as anything for octave material.

" 'Do I use many études, and what?' you ask. Yes, I use quite a number of études, and in a systematic way. I do not accept pupils who have not enough technic to begin with Czerny, Op. 299. After these we take up Czerny, Op. 740, naturally choosing those études which are most suited to the individual. Then we may use some of the Cramer studies, and after these the Clementi *Gradus ad Parnassum*. And finally Chopin, though the Chopin Études can hardly be placed under the heading of studies, as they are really concert pieces.

" 'How early do I use Bach and what selections?' Bach, I consider the spine and body of piano technic and musicianship. In the Cleveland Institute, Bach's compositions are taught from the second year on. I myself do not accept students who are not fitted to begin the Two-part Inventions. Then come the Three-part Inventions. These are followed with the French Suites and Partitas—the English Suites, and then the *Well-tempered Clavichord*. After these—*anything!* Naturally not every student does all these, but the most suitable are used in each instance.

" 'How is one to memorize music—piano music?' I can give you no workable recipe for this. To know something of harmony is a great help. To have absolute pitch, or relatively perfect pitch, is another great help. From the ear to the brain—from the brain to the ear, proves that memory study is a mental process. A person who will practise conscientiously—who thinks what he is doing and uses his mind while he is practising, should have no great difficulty in committing to memory.

" 'How shall the player gain both delicacy and power?'

"Don't you think these things are matters of imagination? Some people are born with them; others must acquire this facility and knowledge —it is never thrust upon one. Power, of course, is merely a matter of the sensible disposition of one's physical forces, under mental control.

" 'How keep technic up to concert pitch?'

"Through practise."

" 'How keep up repertoire?'

"Through more practise.

" 'What technical exercises are a daily necessity for the concert artist?'

"Of course each pianist, each artist, has his own technical forms to fit his special needs. In general, I should say scales, arpeggios, and a judicious selection of Chopin Études."

"Are you in sympathy with modern music?" he was asked. The answer was pithy and to the point—though brief.

"There are, to my thinking, only two sorts of music—good music and bad music. I am in sympathy with good music; I am not in sympathy with bad music!"

An American, born in Georgia—the South is accredited with fostering more ardent temperament than the North—Beryl Rubinstein showed pianistic talent very early, and made his début in concert at the tender age of eight. For six years he continued to play in public, traveling with his father and giving recitals from New York to San Francisco. At fourteen he went to Europe for further study.

Returning to America, the young artist concertized throughout the country, playing in recital and with prominent orchestras. Besides his pianistic gifts, he has developed those of composer and teacher. In the latter capacity he has served for several years as head of the piano department of the Cleveland Institute of Music, in which his success has won wide recognition.

In the line of composition he has produced a piano concerto—played with the Detroit Symphony Orchestra—various songs, a violin sonata, and compositions for the piano. A second violin sonata, also a second piano concerto, are still unpublished.

Added to these various activities—or perhaps in spite of them—the pianist never relaxes his absorbing study of his instrument and its literature. His search for beautiful tone and perfect mechanism has resulted in constant growth. And today Beryl Rubinstein stands an able exponent of beautiful, artistic piano playing.

XXVI

ERNESTO BERUMEN

MIND THE MOTIVE POWER IN PIANO PLAYING

"THERE is one point I should like to emphasize very strongly, and that is the importance—nay, the necessity—of finger technic for the pianist of today." Mr. Berúmen spoke emphatically, and his great dark eyes were serious.

"I think many people are confused nowadays over the numerous piano methods now in vogue. Some of these methods are arbitrary, some diffuse in the extreme; many of them ignore the basic principles of piano technic, so that perhaps it is not to be wondered at that there is an odium attached to the very word—method. To many it stands for something narrow, circumscribed, pedantic. They go to the other extreme and advocate playing without method, just in whatever way is the most natural, especially if one has any talent at all for the piano.

A NATURAL TECHNIC

"Do I believe there is such a thing as a natural technic? I certainly do. But the trouble is that people who are blessed with this sort of technic are not willing to bend down to any sort of technical study. All comes so easy to them that they refuse to be bound by any rules or principles. Whereas I believe that, along with the natural gift, one must labor to perfect it with as much industry as though one were not so gifted."

Ernesto Berúmen is a native of Mexico. He was born in Mazatlán, a town of over 22,000 inhabitants, situated in the extreme western part of the country, near Lower California and the Pacific and within a stone's throw, so to say, from the line of the tropics.

"The people of my country," he says, "are fond of music, but they lack opportunities for serious study, for hearing great artists or for musical cultivation. We have teachers of piano, of course, and it is the fashion for young girls to study a while, until they marry. But they really have not sufficient incentive to carry it further.

"As for myself, I studied music a little, boy fashion, and hoped some day I might become a musician. But my father thought otherwise and sent me to a training school in Los Angeles. Here I also continued my music with an excellent teacher, a lady who taught the Leschetizky principles. She seemed to think music should be my vocation and urged my father to send me abroad as soon as possible. My father finally realized the truth of the matter and after a year spent in Los Angeles, permitted me to go to Europe.

"I went first to Paris and began to work with a pupil of Diémer. I was just a boy, and the gay French capital held many marvels. Perhaps I did not work as seriously as I should have done. At all events, after one year of study in Paris, my father decided to place me in the Leipsic Conservatory. Here I worked very hard under Teichmüller. He is a splendid teacher, most strict and thorough. Here I laid the technical foundation for piano playing and have always been grateful to him for the thoroughness with which it was accomplished. I found later that his ideas of technical development were almost identical with those of Leschetizky.

NECESSITY FOR FINGER TECHNIC

"Teichmüller firmly believed in finger technic and trained his pupils in this from the start. He formed the hand and taught exact movements of the fingers away from the keyboard, on a table, or, to be more exact, on the lid of the piano. 'You get the idea of finger movements and touch as distinct from sound, and your neighbors' ears are spared,' he used to say. He has many unique forms of finger technic passages and chord forms, but has not published a book of exercises as yet, at least so far as I know.

"In 1910 I went to Vienna and played for Leschetizky. He was most kind and invited me to listen to his lessons. I accepted this opportunity and went every afternoon. Sometimes the lessons would extend for five hours. After several months the master, not being very well, went to his summer place at Ischl; he asked me to come to Vienna in the fall. This I thought of doing, but finally decided to return to Leipsic. I could now work much alone and now endeavored to put in practise the ideas I had learned by attending Leschetizky's wonderful classes. For he was so exact and particular about the smallest details. Not about technic, for he left the technical prepartion of students to his Vorbereiters, but about the interpretation and finish of a composition.

"Three years later I returned to America and decided to make my home in New York. I soon began to teach and have been fortunate in having some very talented pupils. What I have just said about finger technic is something I insist on absolutely in my teaching. It seems to me finger technic is being wofully neglected. It is even looked down upon as something old-fashioned and pedantic, as something almost obsolete. People have become obsessed with the idea of relaxation and imagine it will take the place of everything else. They think if they have relaxation it is all they need, and turn a deaf ear to any talk of finger action. I place finger technic first; the pupil must have that; it is an absolute necessity. And he must have it in the beginning, otherwise it is difficult, sometimes impossible, to acquire.

"Following the idea of Teichmüller, I inculcate the principles of finger action away from the keyboard. I also use the Practice Clavier, which I consider a most marvelous invention, a great boon to the pianist, as is also the method used with it. Music students abroad know the little dumb keyboards, often very clumsy affairs, which are in use over there. I was fortunate enough to have a clavier given me while I was in Leipsic. Teichmüller was deeply interested in it, as he had never seen one. He said it carried out his ideas of finger technic admirably.

"As soon as my pupil has an idea what finger action means, and can make good movements, we employ arm movements with relaxed weight. The best way to illustrate this principle—to my thinking—is through chord studies. Of course some relaxed weight attends even finger movements, as the arm is poised on the finger-tips; but the full weight of arm is principally used in chords and octaves. It is so interesting to watch the application of these ideas, and so strange that all teachers do not employ them, for results are so convincing.

TECHNICAL MATERIAL

"As to technical material, I have a set of finger technics I am fond of. They are by Oscar Beringer, of London. They are built on the minor, major and dominant seventh chords and are to be played in all keys. It is true that piano students too often prefer to skim over big piano pieces which make a show, rather than come right down to the foundation and build that up logically and thoroughly. Some, however, are awaking to the fact that they must have technic first, and technic must be applied to smaller pieces before larger ones are attempted. The player must have finger technic for all passages, combined arm, wrist and fingers for melody touch where pressure is used; while for chords the whole weight of arm from shoulder is employed, with arched hand, firm at the knuckles. You thoroughly agree with me, for that is the way you teach yourself. It all seems clear and simple; there is really no reason why students should be mystified. One thing is certain: we cannot do without finger technic; whoever tries to will never acquire what I call a worked-out technic. This means a technic so developed, so controlled and mastered, that the finest effects can be produced at will. I would rather have such a technic than the greatest musical gifts in the world, without it. For the pianistic gift without hard work is a very uncertain quantity, but the worked-out technic can be depended on to carry out the inspiration of the player.

THE NEGLECT OF TECHNIC

"The question is often asked: How shall we induce the piano pupils of today to practise sufficient technic outside of pieces, to play the compositions they study effectively? This seems to be the crying need in piano study. The technical side of the student's study is the side oftenest slighted or left out altogether. All serious teachers of piano, who realize the importance of technical practise outside of pieces, have, no doubt, the same struggle. But in spite of the many difficulties in the way, I insist on daily scale, arpeggio, trill and octave practise. In the case of schoolgirls who claim they cannot devote more than one hour a day to music, I expect them to

give at least one-third of that—twenty minutes
—to scales and other technical material.

SOME CAUSES FOR NEGLECT OF TECHNIC

"There may be several reasons for the failure
to secure necessary technical practise from the
pupil. Let us consider a few.

"First: Indifference of the pupil. American
pupils are considered lazy when it comes to the
study of music. We players and teachers remember, in our student days abroad, how industrious we found the young people over there in
their studies, no matter what the subject. Perhaps that was one benefit the Americans derived
from coming abroad—contact with so much industry. Foreign students set us a good example.
It is quite true we have excellent teachers of
piano in America; there are no finer anywhere in
the world. Why, then, are American students so
indolent and indifferent as to the foundation and
backbone of their musical studies?

"Second: A second difficulty seems to arise
from a misapprehension. The American student
has the mistaken idea that technic practise is
quite unnecessary, despite the fact that his
teacher insists on it. The student attends a
recital by a great piano virtuoso and fancies he

is listening to a genius who never comes down to earth to occupy himself with such humdrum affairs as scales and exercises. He may even inquire of the artist whether he practises 'pure technic' or not, and possibly may receive a negative answer. What of that? The artist will not reveal the weary days, months, years, he has already spent mastering the technic of the piano. If the questioner has no comprehension of the fact, he will not enlighten him. This very thing has happened to me. On one occasion I was asked if I did a great deal of technic practise outside of pieces. Just then I was working over five hours a day on a recital program and wanted to save my strength for that. So I remarked in an offhand way that I was not practising technic just then. Subsequently I heard it said that I disapproved of the practise of pure technic myself and did not do it. You see how false impressions get abroad, for no reason. Have I not practised my head off—excuse the expression—on account of gaining and keeping up an adequate piano technic. One must have a breathing-spell once in a while.

"Third: Is lack of attention to technical practise the fault of the teacher? In looking for reasons why pupils wish to avoid technical study, may not this fact be traced to the teacher, after all? If the teacher gives out as his dictum that all necessary technic can be acquired from pieces, this wipes out all effort in the line of pure technical practise. Thus the indolent pupil has his will: plenty of pieces and no troublesome or stupid scales and exercises. He thinks pieces much more attractive, and naturally has so much more to show for a period of study. He is not bothered with tiresome questions as to *how* he is playing those pieces, or whether he understands the principles underlying the technical problems contained in them. Can we really blame the student for this condition of things?

"The fact remains, however, that the American student of piano seems to avoid technical study whenever possible, for it requires too much thinking. He, therefore, does not lay a dependable foundation, nor make the progress in music that he ought to make. It is up to us teachers to correct this lack as much as in our power lies; we must be a spur and an inspiration to our students, to open his eyes to the needs of the work and urge him on to more faithful study, by showing him how to help himself.

MIND IN PLAYING

"In judging the work of a pianist, one prime factor, one vital force, is apt to be ignored, or but faintly understood. And that vital force is —Mind. You may listen to a player who has an excellent technic and gets over the keys very smoothly and glibly. Yet they always are and remain mere notes, and fail to move you in any way whatsoever. Another pianist will perform the same pieces, but now they glow with life, they are vital in every note; they move you, they carry the message the composer had in mind. The first player thought principally of executing the notes; the second performer used his mental powers to divine the meaning of those notes and made them live again.

"It seems to me that in both teaching and playing we should stress this side of the work—encourage the mental side of piano playing, that we may express what the music means.

"But if we only begin to talk about using mind when teaching pieces, we shall find it difficult to arouse the student to clear thinking. We then realize that the time to use mind was during the technical studies which precede piece playing. The student must form the habit of thinking things out for himself. And the time to acquire this habit is in the working out of technical material given by his teacher. If he never learns to think in these so-called mechanical forms, how shall he be prepared to study into the meaning of a Bach Fugue or a Beethoven Sonata? Music requires more close thinking than almost any other study; that is why it is such splendid mental discipline. There is no use trying to do slipshod, indifferent work in music. If you only have an hour a day to give to music, use every second of that hour with your whole mind.

THE PHRASING OF PIANO MUSIC

"Phrasing is a very wide subject. True there are many editors and many editions of the classics. Perhaps the only criterion to go by is whether the effect of certain punctuation-marks is good, and whether the composition sounds well when played in that way. In the old days there were no fast and fixed rules. The performer, if he were an artist, was free to punctuate the music as he saw fit, just as he was free to use his own ornaments and embellishments. Nowadays we have this or that music editor, whose directions we must perforce follow, if we use his editions. Phrasing signs, to be of value, must be in good taste and should make the piece sound well.

"And a final word. The coming genius of the piano will not be of the sort who will exhibit a more dazzling technic than we have already

known, but rather one who will be able to pene-
trate more deeply into the spirit of music itself,
and have the mind and heart to reveal its spiritual
secrets."

XXVII

RALPH LEOPOLD

PLAYING, TEACHING AND RECORDING EXPERIENCES

THE writer first met Mr. Leopold when he was stationed with Percy Grainger at Governor's Island, serving in the military band. When the necessity for this work was removed, Mr. Leopold was free to resume his profession.

It might be stated at once that this pianist plays the piano as though it were really a musical instrument, to be treated as such. And because of this he draws from his instrument a tone at all times musical. He interprets, too, in a manner at once sane and artistic. These terms betoken sound musicianship.

When questioned as to early musical studies, he said:

"My home was near Philadelphia. I began music at the tender age of six. The organ interested me particularly in those early years, and I had lessons from Frederick Maxon, in Philadelphia, who also taught me some piano. I

secured a church position as organist in Philadelphia as a lad of fifteen. After working along
in this way for a while, I began to realize more
and more that the piano was to be my instrument.
For on the piano one can obtain so much more
tonal variety and tonal coloring; and then its
literature is of such vital, absorbing interest.

"Having made my choice in favor of the piano,
I went abroad for further study. Securing a
teacher in Berlin, I went through a great deal
of material belonging to a pianist's repertoire—
all of which is very necessary to know, of course.
As I became more acquainted with conditions
and also with many students preparing to enter
the concert field, I felt I needed more technical
routine. The second year, therefore, I went to
Leschetizky's representative in Berlin, Mme.
Stepanoff, who gave me exactly what I needed.
I can honestly say I owe most of my progress
and attainments to her wise guidance. For she
taught me how to study. She did not—as so
many artist-teachers do—tell the student to take
this or that piece and bring it to the next lesson.
No, she believed in showing the student how to
study, how to finger and pedal, how to analyze,
how to differentiate the parts, and so on. Thus
I could work intelligently from the start.

"After two years' study, I became Mme.

Stepanoff's assistant. Some of the pupils were prepared by me, while others alternated lessons with us both. Still others were taught entirely by me, many of these being Americans.

"During the last three years of the eight I spent in Germany, I concertized frequently, playing recitals in Munich, Berlin and in many of the larger cities, after making my début in November, 1911, with the Berlin Philharmonic. I returned to America the summer the war broke out, intending to remain but a short time and return, as I had pupils waiting, and a number of concert and recital engagements signed. But conditions became so unsettled that it seemed best to remain in America. Then, when we went into the war, I enlisted, and found my work in the military band. It was delightful to be associated with Percy Grainger, in teaching and drilling the men and arranging music for the different instruments.

PRINCIPLES OF TECHNIC AND PRACTISE

"You ask about my principles of piano technic and practise. I believe most emphatically in exact finger action and finger development; the player can get nowhere without mastering this cardinal point at the very outset. So many players, otherwise ambitious, seem to neglect this important principle, and therefore suffer continuously from the neglect. They may practise the piano for years, then go to an artist-teacher, and still fail to play with good tone and effect. The finishing teacher can spend little time with foundational principles, even if he were willing to do so. The time to learn these principles is in the early stages; yet how few really acquire them! I am very particular about teaching the principles of finger action and articulation, and, of course, I use them myself.

TONE PRODUCTION

"Tone production is one of the most important things. The pupil must be taught to produce a musical tone, to make the tone *sing,* to make it beautiful. To do so the pupil must listen to every note he plays. To get him to listen requires constant vigilance on the part of the teacher. I use many short lyrical pieces to illustrate this; Mendelssohn's *Songs Without Words* are excellent for the purpose.

THE PHRASE

"Then the formation of the phrase must be carefully studied, until the student habitually looks for the form, the punctuation, shading and expression of each theme or portion of melody.

The molding of the phrase can be understood even by young pupils. There is always a note, or notes, that have more stress than others. In general, it is the longer notes that have more pressure than the quicker ones. There is often a slight dwelling on the sustained note of the phrase, which makes the whole more expressive and full of meaning.

TEACHING OCTAVES

"The main thing is a loose, vibrant wrist. I find with pupils that the fifth finger is apt to play much lighter and softer than the thumb. So I endeavor to equalize them by making the fifth finger play up and down the keyboard with light, staccato wrist action, before the hand is stretched to the width of an octave. If the hand is small, an interval of a sixth can be used instead of an eighth, till the span develops.

MEMORIZING

"Just a word on this very large subject. The ear is about the greatest factor. The important thing for the student is to coördinate what she sees on the printed page with its position on the keyboard. The analysis of the piece shows how it is put together, what shape is the melody and what form has the accompaniment, how many measures are alike and how many are different, and many other points. A quick ear is of the greatest help.

DETACHED TOUCH

"As to the French school of detached touch, which seems to attract some players at present, I think one should use this touch very sparingly and with great care. It can be grafted with safety only on a well-developed foundation of articulate finger action. To my thinking it should never be given to a beginner. Indeed common sense proves that if finger action is not understood and practised in the first stages, it is difficult, almost impossible, to acquire it afterward, when movements are more fixed, and habits formed.

KEEPING UP TECHNIC AND REPERTOIRE

"In keeping up technic I am quite free to confess I practise pure technic every day. At least three-quarters of an hour is spent with scales, arpeggios, octaves—and Bach. Besides these, I make technical studies out of difficult passages in pieces. So much can be done with varied accents and rhythms, with use of dynamics and so on.

"In keeping up one's repertoire, pieces should

be reviewed ever so often to keep them in repair. In doing this it is absolutely essential to practise *slowly.* Three times in slow tempo, with careful attention to details, are worth more than a dozen times fast. I take all difficult passages and give them extra attention, working them over slowly.

PIANO RECORDING

"I have always been devoted to Wagner's music dramas ever since I was a child. When I became well enough known as a concert artist to be asked to make records, I found the field for this music was practically open. I set to work to make records of Wagner's *Ring of the Niebelung,* and have made twelve of them. It has been a great pleasure to do them, but I had no idea, when I started in, of the immense amount of labor involved. Yes, it is possible to make recordings that do not take so much of one's time, but I was anxious to have them as nearly perfect as was humanly possible. To accomplish this, one must go over the work a great many times, first for correct notes, then for pedaling, expression, shading and so on.

"I have myself translated—as it were—these themes for voice and orchestra into piano music, trying to give the impression and significance of the original score. I have never written them out, but some day shall probably do so."

Mr. Leopold's first New York recital took place in October, 1919. Since then he has played a number of recitals in New York, besides playing "from coast to coast." He has also appeared with prominent orchestras.

XXVIII

A QUINTET OF BRITISH PIANISTS

EVLYN HOWARD-JONES, HAROLD SAMUEL, KATHARINE BACON, C. SOLOMON, IRENE SCHARRER

WITHIN the last year or two America has become acquainted with several of the later English artists, who have brought to us their art and their manner of playing. For every country has its own sympathies, reactions, ideals of thought and action. And these are revealed in its musical art as well as in its literature, its painting and architecture.

It used to be affirmed that the English are not a musical people, by nature, but this can no longer be said—or thought. Each artist who visits us confirms the impression that all who come from that country are thoroughly schooled, serious musicians. And what good fingers they have! We know before they touch the keys that we shall hear all the notes, and the playing will be sane, well-balanced and orderly. Besides these merits we shall have sentiment and musical insight. Mr. Harold Samuel gave us the inner meaning of Bach; Mr. Howard-Jones seemed equally at home in classic and modern styles; Mr. Solomon revealed the delicate poetic fancy of César Franck; Katharine Bacon fills all she does with womanly charm and Irene Scharrer plays with beauty of tone and distinction of style.

EVLYN HOWARD-JONES

It is a pleasure to record the quick recognition and appreciation this pianist received in both his New York recitals. It was felt that here was a true musical mentality—a pianist "to be reckoned with." It was known that he had played much in England and on the continent; that a season or so ago he had given a series of six consecutive recitals in as many weeks. Ernest Newman wrote that he had played the *Moonlight Sonata* "in a way equal to the best any of the giants have given. For Mr. Howard-Jones has brains, temperament and technic, and the three are happily balanced."

There is nothing exaggerated about the artist, no poses of any kind. Tall and straight, with affable manner, he is always the sincere, unaffected English gentleman. Having but five weeks in all to spend in America and Canada, his time was very limited, but he was willing briefly to discuss his career and ideals.

"I suppose I was what is called a child prodigy," he began. "I had a great love for music, as far back as I can remember, and I was permitted to have piano lessons when I was very small. At the age of nine, I played in a concert. I can recall vividly just how I played—and what. The pieces were Handel's *Harmonious Blacksmith* and Schubert's Impromptu in E flat. Shall I tell you a story about this affair? There were adult singers and instrumentalists who took part. For some unexplained reason, the accompanist left in the middle of the program. The small boy who had just played was asked if he thought he could manage to accompany a singer next on the program. The small boy, with the hardihood of childhood, thought he could. And he did, with the result that he was the accompanist for the rest of the evening.

"My home was in one of the suburbs of London, and I studied piano with a local teacher. As I grew older my desire to become a musician grew also. But my parents had rather puritanical views and did not favor my devoting myself to music.

"One day I decided to take matters into my own hands. I presented myself at the Royal

Academy of Music and won a three years' scholarship. Here I had Franklin Taylor for piano, a pianist and teacher of the old school, very strict and severe. He seemed to belong to a past age, for we, in these days, look at technic from another viewpoint. Not as a continual grind of exercises and études, but rather, through understanding underlying principles, as forming a reliable foundation to support the superstructure to be built upon it.

"After finishing at the Academy, I played in concert and taught. As soon as I was able, I traveled. Before very long I was in Berlin and studying with Eugen d'Albert. A good teacher? A great musical personality, from association with whom one could learn much.

"After a time I returned to London and was active in both playing and teaching. I held professorships in various schools and colleges. Then came the war, which disrupted much of the musical life of our country and turned it into different channels. For this and other reasons I gave up the schools where I was teaching to devote myself more exclusively to recitals and to private pupils. I have some excellent talents in my care, some of whom you will no doubt hear of before very long.

"As for my own development, I will say that

I am responsible for much of it. One can acquire certain things from teachers, but must work out the major portion one's self. My platform experience has taught me much. Doing the thing in public, before others, is a great teacher. And it is a good thing for any one—teacher or player —to keep always at his own study, always learning new works, always experimenting. Even if not actually appearing in public, keep ready to do so—don't fall behind.

MOST IMPORTANT THING IN TEACHING

"About the most important thing in teaching is to get the pupil to listen—to hear what he is himself doing. This requires close concentration, naturally, but this he must also learn. If the student can sing, even a little, or play on some stringed instrument, in each case he is obliged to follow the theme or tune in a single voice, which helps his ear very much and his perception of the melodic line. All these things make for more thorough musicianship.

TECHNICAL MATERIAL

"I do not believe in a lot of cumbersome material—masses of études and vain repetition of scales. These waste a great deal of time and can become so automatic that the player can read a book while his fingers run scales! Do nothing without thought, for the work should be—and is —entirely mental. My idea is to have a few technical forms, carefully thought out and understood. Technic need never make one mechanical, as some teachers think. The scale form is simple enough; so is the arpeggio. Trills and chords are not difficult to comprehend, if correctly presented. Czerny, Op. 740, contains about everything in the way of technical problems, and the study may be carried further in the études of Clementi, Henselt and Moscheles.

UNPREPARED PUPILS

"In the case of pupils who have been playing too difficult pieces without proper foundation, I try to awaken their musical sense, also their listening sense, so that they realize they are not making good tones. Then I show them why this is so. I hardly think it a good plan to take away all piece playing from them, for any length of time, lest they become disheartened and fall back into mere mechanical ways. I would always have them play some small pieces. The pieces can be very simple ones, in which they can apply the principles I am giving, and can experiment with them.

ON MEMORIZING

"There are three ways of committing a piece to memory: through the eye, or the visual; through the ear, or the aural; and through the fingers, or muscular memory. A close analysis of the piece as to its keys and harmonic progressions is necessary, also as to its form and structure. As to the work in detail, I should advise reading the piece through a number of times away from the piano; very much of the physiognomy and content can be discovered in this way. Then take a small portion at a time, study each hand alone, then hands together. Proceed in this way until the whole is learned. After this comes the experimenting as to whether you have the piece securely under control under all conditions. For this security, experience on the concert platform is most valuable, for it is a test of what you have accomplished.

"You have a wonderful musical atmosphere in this great music center by the sea. Last week there were four splendid orchestras giving concerts on consecutive evenings—the Philadelphia, the Philharmonic, the New York, and the Boston Symphonies. I attended all but the first; as for the Philadelphia, there was no seat to be had for love or money.

"I have greatly enjoyed my short stay here, and hope to return next season."

HAROLD SAMUEL

From his London managers come these bits of information of Harold Samuel: "Born in London; educated at Royal College of Music, with Dannreuther and Stanford, also had lessons with Albeniz, Spanish composer. Principally known from his playing of Bach. His feat—which no other pianist ever attempted—of giving six Bach recitals on six consecutive days, made a stir in the world of music. Has published many songs and a comic opera, and has played in many countries."

"I am immensely interested in Harold Samuel and believe he is bound to make a success wherever he is heard. He started his career as an accompanist and proved to be first-rate. He accompanied me many times, and I came to know him well. Knowing his fondness for Bach's music, I suggested one day that he should present himself to the public as a Bach player. He demurred at first, but I kept at him until he gave a Bach program, which proved to be a unique success. He can now announce a week of Bach recitals in London, giving one each day, and be sure of a crowded hall. All of which proves that my estimate of his powers was correct." So spoke his fellow-artist and friend, Fraser Gange, the distinguished Scotch baritone.

Mr. Samuel paid a flying visit to the United States, making his début at the Berkshire Festival in 1924, and subsequently playing a couple of recitals in New York and Boston. In a conversation in Pittsfield, during Festival days, the pianist said:

"The first thing people usually say to me is: 'So you play everything of Bach!' While I am familiar with most of Bach's music, I cannot say I have learned it all. Who could? Of the Forty-eight Preludes and Fugues of the *Well-tempered Clavichord*, perhaps I have half that number at my finger-ends. I may have an even greater number of works by Beethoven and Schumann in memory, but people associate me with Bach's music and call for that.

"My early piano studies were made with Edward Dannreuther. In America he may be known principally by his writings on music, but he was really a fine musician, pianist, teacher and lecturer. He had studied under Richter and Moscheles in Leipsic. As a pianist he introduced Chopin's F minor Concerto in London, also Liszt's two Concertos, the Grieg in A minor and the Tschaikowsky in B flat minor. He was a teacher of high aims and solid attainments, and believed in thorough technical foundation. I was trained in Czerny, Tausig, Clementi, and even old Plaidy came in for a share of attention.

"In my own teaching I do not use Plaidy, Hanon or Pischna, but do use much Czerny, such as Ops. 299, 740 and a few others. Scales we cannot do without, either, nor other forms of pure technic. One must have very even, exact finger articulation in order to play clearly and effectively. All these things must be carefully studied by the pupil. Sometimes we try to sugar-coat the pill by giving a piece containing the difficulty. Then, when the pupil finds she cannot master the problem, she is willing to work at the technical steps which lead to the solution.

"You speak of Matthay. A great teacher—one of the greatest we have. He has trained some splendid artists. Think of Myra Hess, a superb player. Like Novaes you say? I haven't heard the young Brazilian since she has matured. As a young girl I remember she had enormous talent. She must be one of the elect. Hess is well known in America. Matthay is responsible for other artists, among them Irene Scharrer, perhaps a little less militant than Hess, but very gifted.

"No, I have never played in South America,

but have appeared in South Africa. Of course, the cities there are not very large, at least not to a New Yorker. At Cape Town and Johannesburg I had good audiences, and the people seemed to understand what I was trying to do.

BASIS OF TECHNIC

"The basis of all piano technic is the fact that it is a mental function before it becomes a physical one. Consequently, whether one aims at the bettering of one's *staccato,* or the improvement of one's *arpeggios,* there should be a very definite plan of campaign in the mind, before one touches the keyboard at all. To illustrate this point, I would point out the benefit arising from examining a point of difficulty in a work, without playing it, in order to discover what may stand in the way of successful achievement.

FINGER ACTION

"You ask me about finger action. There are too many things connected with it to particularize just now. But the student who aims at *independence* must try and get out of his—or her —head the so-called fact that every species of finger touch is *composite,* as this idea may tend to lack of crispness. On the other hand, an attempt to *isolate* the action by *tensing* the hand

and arm, will result in that rigidity which every pianist is taught in these days to avoid. Let the student always remember that the hand and arm can be quiet without any appreciable muscular effort, and that any kind of holding is fatal to that ease and freedom which are so necessary to attain and so hard to get.

"I think it very easy to stress technic too much and to regard it as the end, instead of realizing it only as a means to the end.

CLASSIC OR MODERN MUSIC

"I cannot specify that any particular works of any master are my favorites. I always get excited about the last thing I am playing. Perhaps I enjoy playing the music of Bach, Mozart, Scarlatti, Brahms, Beethoven and Debussy, in preference to others, but it is very difficult to say, because there is so much to enjoy in so many others."

KATHARINE BACON

When a young artist has given ten recitals of her own in New York, in the short space of three years, and each one with success, it behooves music lovers to consider who it is who holds such a record. When we know that the programs played in those ten recitals of piano music covered a wide range of styles, from classic to ultra-modern, we realize that this pianist must have wedded her natural musical gifts with a talent for hard work, in order to have accomplished so much in such a comparatively short time.

Katharine Bacon, the young English pianist referred to, was chatting in my studio one afternoon, and was led to tell something of her story.

"I must have been extremely fond of music from babyhood, because an old friend of our family gave me a few lessons when I was about four. Then, somewhat later, I had lessons from a lady teacher, but think I could not have learned very much from her, for she was not very strict. In the matter of fingering, she would allow me to use whatever fingers I chose. The only discipline I had was playing a few scales. I had learned to read quite quickly, for a small child, so devoured everything I could pick up in the way of a tune or a piece. When I found one that pleased my fancy, I would take it to my teacher, saying I wanted to learn that instead of the music which had been given me to study.

"When I was nine I began to study more seriously—this time with one of the best organists of our home town—Chesterfield. This man, though really an organist, was a good musician, and I learned much from him about music, and was with him over two years.

"Then, one day, Arthur Newstead, pianist and teacher of London, came to Chesterfield to give a recital, and I was taken to hear him. After the recital I met the artist and was asked to play for him. It was an exciting event for a small child to walk out on the platform he had just left and play on the very same piano he had used but a few moments before. I was but a mite of a girl, small for my age; but he was very kind and said I had talent.

"And now came the time when it was decided I must advance in my studies and broaden my outlook. Arthur Newstead was consulted. He said he would teach me if I could come to London for my lessons. This I did, making the round-trip of three hundred miles, from Chesterfield to London and back, twice a week, for four years. Naturally, I studied very hard, and feel I owe everything to my teacher—now my husband—who practically made a pianist of me. I often feel so grateful for the advantage of having been trained by one teacher, instead of running around to this one and that. To me it does not seem a good plan for the student to frequently change teachers; for the teacher it is also detrimental, as he has not the time to prove what he can do for the pupil.

"My teacher was anxious to become professionally acquainted with America and accepted an appointment at the Peabody Conservatory in Baltimore. I followed shortly after and continued my studies with him. Two years later we were married. For the last four or five years New York has been our home.

"In regard to playing in public, I have always done considerable of it. Even in my home town, as a child, I used to play at concerts and give recitals. In Baltimore, while living there, I gave a series of recitals each year. At one of these series I gave the last five Sonatas of Beethoven, one on each program. Yes, I have studied through much piano literature.

"How do I memorize? Very easily and quickly; it seems to come naturally to me. One thing that helps greatly is that I read at sight so quickly. In taking up a new piece, I first play it through to get something of its plan and meaning before beginning to study it. I can often commit to memory a long and difficult work in a week or less."

In the summer of 1925 the young artist returned to her homeland for a vacation, but at the same time combined business with pleasure, for she played in various concerts and recitals. This led to about twenty concert engagements in England for the following winter, which she left her work in America to fulfill. She is fast attaining her musical stature and forging to the front.

MR. C. SOLOMON

As one of the younger of the gifted British pianists who have come to us, Mr. Solomon disclosed his art in two very interesting recitals, with excellent programs. An intimate chat with the artist disclosed some of his aims and ideals.

"I studied in London with Dr. Rumschisky, and found him a most excellent teacher in every way; he did a great deal for me. He is residing in America at the present time. I studied with him for nearly three years. Later on, in order to have a broader outlook, I went to Paris; was with Cortot for a while and then with Lazare-Lévy for two years. After this came much playing in various parts of Europe. I am now living in London, playing much and also teaching. I am deeply interested in my work and have some very talented pupils.

EXPRESSING THOUGHT THROUGH THE FINGERS

"One phase of playing and teaching has impressed me, and that is the wide discrepancy between what the student has in mind and what she really says with her fingers. She may love music and may have a creditable idea of the meaning of the piece she is playing. She may imagine she is expressing those ideas in her playing, but she is far from doing so. I say to her: 'What does the music mean to you? Have you formed a mental concept of its idea or story? If you think you have expressed these ideas in your playing you are quite mistaken, for I heard only notes.' This is quite a new idea to her; it is a surprise to find she is not expressing her thought through her fingers.

"Yes, I believe there are touches on the piano that express different qualities of thought, feeling and emotion, such as gayety or sorrow, brightness or despair. I know this is a very elusive subject and can hardly be put into words. It can only be experienced and worked out by each player individually.

MANY RIGHT WAYS

"We so often hear it said there's only one right way to play a passage or piece, though there may be many wrong ways. I often feel like reversing this dictum by saying there are several right ways and only one wrong way. That is to say, if the way you are doing has nothing in common with any of the right ways, it surely must be wrong. On the other hand, if there were but one right way, how monotonous! Where would there be a place for individuality? Ask four or five great pianists to play the same work and will not each one render it a little differently from all the others? Each will express *himself;* he cannot help doing so if he is truly sincere.

WHAT IS TRADITION?

"We hear, too, much about tradition in piano playing. What is tradition, anyway? How have these laws become crystallized around the music of Bach, of Beethoven, of Chopin—that these composers must be played in just a certain way? Who says they must be?

"To be sure, we feel the music of Haydn and Mozart expresses beauty for its own sake—simple beauty and charm. So tradition says it must be played with simplicity. Well and good. But one man's idea of simplicity may not be that of other men. And so we can have much diversity, within bounds, as it were. It is the same with

Beethoven, Schumann, Brahms and the moderns. Even if critics do prate of tradition, we must still be able to express our individuality—within reason. Otherwise piano playing would descend to the level of hidebound so-called tradition.

THE TECHNICAL SIDE

"In teaching technic, I try to have the pupil do everything with ease—with the least effort. I avoid excessively high finger action. Some teachers make so much of the up-motion; I make more of the down. It's not up, up, up, but down, down, *down.* To be sure, one must be up in order to come down, but the *down* is the end and aim in view.

"The first aim is to teach a pure legato. Many think they are playing legato when they are not. And no doubt the effort to lift the fingers high is the cause of much of the strain that prevents a pure legato.

ILLUSTRATING LEGATO

"I play a *glissando* up the keyboard, for instance, using the middle fingers of the right hand. As you see, it is perfectly simple, effortless, and is a real legato; it illustrates what I mean. Following out this idea of one tone melting into another, without the slightest break between them, I teach the scale in the same way. And, though you will not agree, perhaps, I allow the student to overlap the tones a little, in order to secure the legato I seek. This, of course, can be modified later.

MODERN MUSIC

"Do I play modern music? I play so little of it that I can say with truth, 'No, I do not.' It seems to me a pianist who will play Bach, Mozart, Beethoven, Schumann, Chopin and a few others, has his heart and hands full of what is most beautiful in musical art. It is time lost to study what has no lasting beauty and stability; which makes no appeal to one's higher nature. No, I have not yet played MacDowell's music, though I am a little familiar with some of the shorter pieces, and have looked through some of the Sonatas, but have never heard them played."

IRENE SCHARRER

THE GIFT OF RETENTIVE MEMORY

To hear Irene Scharrer play is to listen to an artist whose fluent technic and beautiful variety of tone are used to convey the poetic conceptions of an intensely musical nature. Her appearances in America have given sincere pleasure to musicians and students alike.

To come into friendly intercourse with this London pianist is to meet with a sweet, winsome personality of great charm. Her unassuming cordiality attracts at once, and we were soon chatting like old friends.

"You know," she began, "that I am a pupil of Matthay in London, and owe every bit of what success I have gained to him. I am so glad you know him also. He takes the deepest interest in all his pupils, not only in their musical progress, but in every other way. He treats us as though we were his children, and we look up to him as to a father.

"I especially feel this kind regard for him, as my mother was herself a pupil of his. She began to teach me the piano when I was only five years old, and brought me to Matthay when I was ten. After close study with him for six years, I made my début in London at sixteen. Since then I have played much in England and on the continent both in recital and with orchestra.

"In the matter of technic itself, I had to do a great deal of it in early years. Whoever takes the Royal Academy exams.—as I have—must master every variety of scale, arpeggio, trill, octaves and all the rest. As for études—other than those of Chopin—I have only done a few of Czerny. But those wonderful Chopin studies!

They meet the pianist's every need. There are scale and arpeggio passages, trills, double thirds and double sixths, octaves, chromatics—in short, everything one can think of. And best of all, when through their study one is developing one's technic to the virtuoso stage, one is at the same time learning beautiful works of art that can be used on any program. I have frequently given an 'all Chopin' program, and love to do it.

"You ask how I memorize my repertoire. I am frequently asked this question, and it troubles me that I cannot give a really satisfactory answer. The absolute truth is, I don't know exactly how I do it. It seems to come of itself. I know the ear plays a major rôle, for I hear the music mentally. Some others commit music through the eye, and can see the notes on the printed page as they play. Of the three ways often spoken of—the ear, eye, and hand—I consider the last very unreliable; if one trusts too much to it one is sure to make shipwreck in some way. In my case it is the ear I depend on to carry me through.

"One fortunate thing about my memory work is that I retain what I memorize indefinitely. I can remember the tiny tunes I had to write as a little girl. On one occasion I told Myra Hess that I could still recall the first little tune she wrote—we all had to do them then. She had quite forgotten these early efforts, but I still remembered them. I can recall the first piece I ever played in public.

"This gift—if it be that—of retentive memory, is a wonderful help in keeping up repertoire. On some occasions I have to play a recital with almost no time to prepare, or must appear with orchestra at a few hours' notice and without rehearsal. But the pieces are so fixed in mind that I don't forget them. Do not imagine from this that I merely have to play over the piece a few times in order to know it by heart. That would be too superficial. Of course I analyze the piece and work it out in sections."

The two concertos which the young artist played in America—the Schumann with the Boston Symphony, under Koussewitzky, and Beethoven's No. 4, in New York, were discussed. Miss Scharrer has a deep affection for each of these works. The Beethoven is more spiritual, she feels; the Schumann more human. The one touches lofty mountain peaks, where Beethoven dwelt in sublime moments; the other reveals a tender romantic nature, pondering problems of the heart.

THE END

DATE

GAYLORD